Antoni Gaudí

T0274824

Titles in the series Critical Lives present the work of leading cultural figures of the modern period. Each book explores the life of the artist, writer, philosopher or architect in question and relates it to their major works.

In the same series

Antoni Gaudí

Michael Eaude

REAKTION BOOKS

For Marisa, with love, who like me overcame early indifference, even aversion, and came to appreciate Gaudí's genius

Published by Reaktion Books Ltd
Unit 32, Waterside
44–48, Wharf Road
London N1 7UX, UK
www.reaktionbooks.co.uk

First published 2024
Copyright © Michael Eaude 2024

Printed and bound in Great Britain by Bell & Bain, Glasgow

A catalogue record for this book is available from the British Library

ISBN 978 1 78914 837 4

Contents

Antoni Gaudí in the Sagrada Família, Barcelona, 1916.

Introduction

Antoni Gaudí is a legendary figure and many of the stories about him are just that: legends. He wrote only one newspaper article in his life, published no books and led so private a private life that most of the hundreds of people who write about him retail gossip or clutch at rumours. When one reads the numerous books about his life and work, details are often contradictory. As he had no children, no wife or partner and no surviving siblings, most of the pithy or oracular sayings attributed to Gaudí were written down years later by younger admirers, making them necessarily at one remove from what he actually said.

Where he is known, with no possible contradiction, is in his buildings. In 1984, UNESCO declared three of Gaudí's creations, all in Barcelona, World Heritage Sites: Park Güell, the Palau Güell and the Casa Milà. In 2005, this selection was expanded to include four more: in Barcelona, the Casa Vicens, the Nativity facade and Crypt of the Sagrada Família temple, the Casa Batlló and, in the nearby town of Santa Coloma de Cervelló, the Crypt of the Colònia Güell. Altogether, these seven buildings are known as the Works of Antoni Gaudí, which, according to UNESCO, 'reflect an eclectic, very personal style to which Gaudí gave free rein in the field of architecture, as well as in the design of gardens, sculptures, and indeed all the arts'.[1]

The phrase 'indeed all the arts' makes me smile, for it seems like a verbal shrug of the shoulders: how can we define this man? Gaudí was a total architect: he designed the building and was there (in most cases) chopping and changing it throughout the construction.

Sagrada Família, 2022, with the shining star in place on the Virgin Mary tower.

He designed the tiling, the wallpaper, the window recesses, the doors and their handles, the roof, the furniture and the garden. Architecture, interior design, sculpture – 'all the arts'.

Gaudí was an even more contradictory character than most of us: spending nothing on his own food, clothes or housing, yet huge sums on buildings paid for by others; a revolutionary architect, but deeply conservative in his politics; a disappointed man in his personal life, lonely and possessed of the morbid religious belief that bodily suffering was good, yet creator of passionate architecture full of colour and joy. He believed in order, hierarchy and patriarchal tradition, but his artistic imagination was free, chaotic and eclectic. Austere as a saint in his old age, he raised buildings that were extravagant in three senses: huge in size, costing a fortune and overflowing with extraordinary detail and colour.

Yet if one looks at him from another angle, he was consistent – in his extremism. In almost everything Gaudí did, his commitment was total. He rode roughshod over city planners and even the wishes of his clients to build what he wanted. He was so Catalanist that he insisted on talking in Catalan to the police of a Spanish dictatorship hostile to Catalan, getting himself arrested. He became so deeply religious that he nearly fasted to death. He was so committed to the Sagrada Família basilica that he ended up sleeping in its workshop. He believed pedestrians should have right of way over traffic, so refused to look when he stepped off pavements. Gaudí was a fanatic, though this assertion should be nuanced with another smile, for there is humour and irony, too, in Gaudí, seen in numerous personal exchanges or in the animals peeking out from the corners of his buildings.

The many reminiscences of the young adulators who knew Gaudí in the last two decades of his life are unreliable. These tend to emphasize his religious nature, isolation and apartness from society. This is not a wholly true picture. As a younger man he was something of a dandy, possibly an atheist and an organizer of the Rambling Association. He made many friends. And even in those last two decades he maintained close friendships and worked with a great many associates, fellow architects and numerous artisans and employees. He was never absent from public life: he attended religious processions and Catalanist demonstrations right up to the end of his days. He was a strong believer in Church intervention in civil society.

There were three main strands to Gaudí's thought: he was extremely right-wing, a fervent Catalanist and a militant Catholic. His reactionary nationalism and religious fanaticism were both exacerbated as he aged, by disappointment at a country dominated from Madrid and hatred for an increasingly godless society in which anarchists led a powerful working class.

This short biography follows the arc of his life: his childhood in rural Riudoms and the commercial city of Reus in southern Catalonia; his student years in Barcelona in the 1870s, deeply affected by the deaths of most of his family members; his fateful meeting with Eusebi Güell, who became his friend and main patron; his first contracts; his profound midlife religious crisis in the 1890s; then his greatest, most glorious civil buildings in the 1900s, when the eclecticism of his early years fused into a new, original

Torre Bellesguard.

and inimitable style; and his last decade and a half devoted to the Sagrada Família basilica.

The book examines, too, the various influences on Gaudí, both the social and political ones, such as the Catalan national Renaixença or rebirth (embraced) and the rise of anarchism (abhorred), and the multiple artistic ones: the international art nouveau movement; Catalan Gothic and Moorish architecture; Eugène Viollet-le-Duc, who asked architects to dismember old buildings to see how they worked and use modern techniques to improve Gothic; the new and open-minded Barcelona School of Architecture; the Orientalism of the painter Marià Fortuny, also from his native Reus like so many of Gaudí's colleagues; the Arts and Crafts movement associated with William Morris; and John Ruskin's rejection of mass-produced goods, even though the money that paid for Gaudí's clients' buildings came from the Industrial Revolution.

We can analyse the buildings of this strange man and look at his influences and his social context, and to do this is essential and interesting. His genius is harder to define; it cannot be totally explained. You have to go to Barcelona and feel his buildings, for beyond everything there is an instinct at play: the instinct of just where to place that brick or that space. Nothing like Gaudí's greatest buildings had been seen before. This book is a small introduction to this completely original architect, a revolutionary with roots in the oldest traditions.

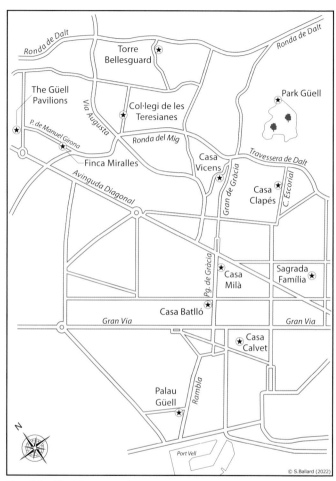

Map of Gaudí buildings in Barcelona.

1

Watching Nature Twist and Turn

Reus is a small city in southern Catalonia, just 11 kilometres (7 mi.) inland from its twin and rival city, Tarragona, which was the capital of Roman Iberia and is famous now for its magnificent Roman monuments. Reus today is known to British holidaymakers as the airport for the Costa Daurada, particularly the resort of Salou with its golden sands.

Antoni Gaudí i Cornet, the future architect, was born there on 25 June 1852 – or perhaps in Riudoms, a village 5 kilometres (3 mi.) from Reus. His father, Francesc Gaudí, was a coppersmith in Reus, while the family of Antoni's mother, Antònia Cornet, were also coppersmiths, in Riudoms. The Gaudí-Cornet family had two houses in Reus and two in Riudoms. Antoni, the fifth and last child of his parents, born when they were both aged 39, was baptized in Reus, but there is no agreement on his exact birthplace. He was probably born at the Mas de la Calderera (Woman Boilermaker's Farmhouse), his mother's family home in Riudoms, and was baptized the next day at Sant Pere church in Reus. The house stands on the outskirts of Riudoms, on the Reus side of the village.

The young Antoni growing up in Reus and Riudoms could not avoid living through the political turbulence of his time, occurring when he was at a particularly impressionable age. Spain's Queen Isabella II was deposed in 1868. The main architect of this progressive coup d'état that lifted censorship, legalized trade unions and inspired Republican fervour was General Joan Prim, a native of Reus and one of the few Catalans ever to preside over the Spanish government. Prim arranged the coming of a new king, Amadeo of Savoy, but was

Mas de la Calderera, Riudoms. Gaudí's probable birthplace.

assassinated in Madrid on the snowy night of 27 December 1870. Amadeo reached Spain a few days later and never settled after this ill-omened start. He resigned in February 1873, finding it impossible 'to govern so profoundly disturbed a country'.[1] His abdication led to the First Republic of 1873–4, followed by the restoration of the Bourbon monarchy in the form of Isabella's son, Alfonso xii, in 1874. All this political upheaval was played out against the background of the Third Carlist War (1872–6), with battles and skirmishes in the mountains of the Priorat, inland from Reus.

Antoni was also keenly aware of his city's history. Reus in the nineteenth century was no backwater but a thriving commercial and industrial centre, the second city of Catalonia after Barcelona. The 1820 census gave it 25,500 inhabitants. 'This modern busy manufacturing town is in perfect contrast with desolate decaying Tarragona,' wrote the English traveller Richard Ford in the 1840s.[2] *Aiguardent*, 'firewater', a rough brandy distilled from the lees of the grape juice used to make wine, was Reus's most famous product, exported through the port of Salou all over Europe and to America. Reus also exported leather, silk, cotton, hazelnuts and olive oil.

Salou had become Reus's main port because the Archbishopric of Tarragona levied too heavy a tax on the *aiguardent* produced in Reus. This prompted Reus's burghers to seek an independent outlet to the sea by building a canal to Salou. In 1804 the central government granted permission, as long as Reus paid for it. Local businesses raised the money, but then Napoleon's 1808 invasion meant that the capital collected for the canal was seized by the government for military purposes.

This theft was key to Reus being more self-consciously and assertively Catalan than Tarragona. Its nineteenth-century business wealth and Spain's appropriation of its canal cash meant that the city felt keenly, and before other parts of Catalonia, the negative effects of an impoverished central state. Reus was a modern, commercial city, fed up with both the Carlist strongholds that waged trade-damaging war in the nearby hills and a Madrid without the money to develop infrastructures. Antoni's childhood and youth were marked by this business-minded and fiercely Catalanist city.

The family suffered private sadness, not uncommon at the time but no less sad. Antoni's oldest sibling, Rosa, was not strong, and the second and third of the five children, Maria and Francesc, died aged four and two. Antoni himself was often unwell, suffering severe pains, diagnosed sometimes as arthritic, sometimes as rheumatic, from the age of five. These attacks, interspersed with periods of remission, affected him all his life. At times he had to ride to school on a donkey instead of walking. He grew, both coddled by his family and aware of his parents' grief and life's fragility. Unlike his brother Francesc (baptized with the same name as his deceased brother), who ran free through the fields of Riudoms, Antoni could often only sit and watch. He became the child-observer. One of his recent biographers, Joan Castellar-Gassol, imagines lyrically what the child could see in the pre-industrial countryside of the Mas de la Calderera, the farm at Riudoms:

> Spiders were master-builders who constructed bridges over rivers . . . The shells of snails had fascinating spiral shapes . . . The rough trunks of the olive trees also twisted themselves into spirals.[3]

From early childhood, Antoni had the opportunity to see how nature avoids straight lines.

Something else twisted in his childhood. The family of Antoni's mother Antònia, his father Francesc and his grandfathers were all coppersmiths. They made boilers, stills (for the *aiguardent*) and copper pipes. The pipes that ran in and out of stills were called *serpentines*, as they turned and twisted like serpents. Antoni spent many hours in his family's workshops observing how hammers and heat turned flat metal into curved, three-dimensional shapes. It was an abiding influence: the architect Gaudí is known for his grasp of curves and three-dimensionality. The architect he was to become saw in three dimensions. It is often said he could not draw. This is untrue – he could and did, though later he delegated drawing to assistants – but he preferred three-dimensional models of his buildings.

Antoni attended a primary school in Reus from 1861 to 1863. It was run by the father of Francesc Berenguer (1866–1914), who, though fourteen years younger than Gaudí, would become a close friend and a collaborator on several projects in Barcelona.

Desolate Monastery

From 1863 to 1868, Gaudí attended the Escola Pia (Piarist School) in Reus. Here Antoni was an average student, only excelling in geometry. He failed several exams. Castellar-Gassol summed up the adolescent's character, highlighting traits that would define Gaudí all his life:

> He was still subject to rheumatic pains, and his character – independent, withdrawn, stubborn and reflective – was not given to the collective discipline nor the systematic routine of education.[4]

He made, though, two good friends, Josep Ribera and Eduard Toda, with whom he spent his leisure time on long walks. They investigated the Roman ruins in Tarragona, all dust and crumble then, nothing like today's restored marvels. Castellar-Gassol quotes the memoirs of Toda, who became a well-known Egyptologist:

> The three friends had one common interest: walking in the fields, contemplating ancient remains in the area. In particular they sought out evocative spots that would stimulate their romantic imagination.[5]

There was nothing unusual in adolescents and young men of the time walking all over Catalonia, especially up its mountains. Even today, at weekends the hills of Catalonia are packed with ramblers, women as well as men now, often belonging to clubs. On the one hand, the long history of political repression has led people to the mountains, where the Catalan language could be freely spoken and dissident ideas unheard by the police. On the other hand, the hill-climbing reiterated pride in the country's remarkable beauty. Gaudí and his friends combined the physical freedom and joys of mountain-walking with the intellectual pleasure of finding out about their country's past.

In Gaudí's time, the Catalan Renaissance was in the air. After the crushing of Catalan rights following defeat in the War of the Spanish Succession in 1714, by the mid-nineteenth century Catalan language, culture and politics were in the first flush of a resurgence, known as the Renaixença (Renaissance or Rebirth), which had a profound influence on Gaudí's thinking. He became a Catalan nationalist, rejecting that his country should be governed so strictly from Madrid.

The rambling of Gaudí and his friends also encompassed Catalonia's medieval monuments, which to a nationalist's eye emphasized what a great country it had once been. Gaudí and his friends hunted down Roman ruins and medieval castles and discovered the monastery of Poblet, not so far from Reus. Poblet is the great Cistercian monastery in honey-coloured stone where the ancient Counts of Barcelona, the Catalan monarchs, were buried. Among the eight alabaster royal tombs, hanging in a double row above head height, is that of Peter the Great, sovereign of the Crown of Aragon,[6] who conquered Sicily in the thirteenth century.

Plundered in 1812 by Napoleon's Marshal Suchet, Poblet was then sacked by its furious peasants in 1835, anticipating the 1836–7 dissolution of monasteries. Emptied of monks, it sunk into further decay. Augustus Hare, a visitor in 1871 – just a couple of years after Gaudí, Ribera and Toda – found donkeys tied up by the broken tombs of kings. Wilfully ignorant of the feudal powers of the monastery over its peasants that had provoked their destructive vengeance, Hare stormed:

> It is the very abomination of desolation . . . the most utterly ruined ruin that can exist . . . where the outer coverings of the walls have been violently torn away, and where the marble pillars and beautiful tracery lie dashed to atoms upon the ground.'[7]

The seventeen-year-old Gaudí and his friends were shocked at this 'utterly ruined ruin'. Founded in the twelfth century, Poblet had been a great centre of learning and wealth, with control over ten towns and many more villages. The monastery's physical size reflected its importance as one of Catalonia's outstanding monuments, alongside the abbey at Ripoll in the Pyrenees or the complex of buildings around Barcelona's Plaça del Rei. The art critic Robert Hughes wrote: 'As architecture, Poblet was the grandest expression of the Cistercian strain in medieval Catalunya, strong, severe, and plain, with prismatic forms and daringly vaulted spaces.'[8] When Gaudí found it, the tombs had been opened (it was falsely believed that kings were buried with treasure), paintings stolen, books damaged, stones removed for other buildings. Toda said later it reminded them of the City of Desolation. Gaudí and his friends were not insulated from the political upheavals of the time. These were Catalan nationalist children, who saw in Poblet's plight the decadence of their nation. They were also Catholic children, living through the social upheaval and ferment of ideas after the overthrow of the monarchy, when Catholic ideas were questioned.

Toda, Ribera and Gaudí formulated the enormous project of rebuilding and repopulating Poblet. They were reaching back into Catalonia's medieval greatness to find its Christian roots while formulating utopias of how its future could be. The teenagers' drawings and writings on Poblet survive. Curiously, some are written on the backs of leaflets produced by the 'Federal Republican Committee of Reus', probably belonging to Toda's radical uncle, who was the president of this committee, set up in 1868 on the fall of the monarchy. These drawings and writings illustrate both the fantasy and the obsessive detail that were to characterize Gaudí's later work.

In 1867 or 1869, the three schoolboys stayed for several weeks of the summer holidays at the house of Ribera's uncle, the schoolteacher at Espluga de Francolí, under an hour's walk from Poblet, to work on their project. Though their writings described the dire state of the ruin and criticized harshly the liberals they saw as responsible for this state of affairs, they did not argue for a restored monastery. Rather, they planned an ideal, cooperative community of artists and artisans.

The school friends projected in detail rail and road communications and planned for Poblet a museum (exhibits specified), an art gallery, a souvenir shop and a café with a billiards table. How to pay for it? They hoped that the workers would live and eat communally at the monastery they were restoring, so saving on wages. Their ideas were idealistic and hardly practical, but they echoed the lives of the monks and lay brothers who had lived there and also reflected the progressive cooperatives of the time. This would be a strand in the austere and rather lonely Gaudí: his liking for communal life, whether in monasteries, in the Mataró cooperative or the later design of the Güell industrial village, even though he himself never lived in this way. The friends planned, too, to charge visitors an entrance fee. They were, surprisingly, anticipating the arrival of tourism in a Spain that was still very much off the Grand Tour of rich North Europeans.

In the friends' plans, Gaudí would be responsible for the physical rebuilding of the monastery. The author of this century's most complete book in English on Gaudí, Gijs van Hensbergen, speculates:

For Gaudí, it provided his first architectural laboratory, offering the chance to unpick 'little portions' of the buildings to see how they worked. What percentage of rubble to facing stone was used in a flying buttress? How heavy was a keystone? Gaudí was fascinated by the structural hints revealed, that the 'nudity of the beggar is seen through his rags'.[9]

They calculated the water needed, the quarries for the stone and the number of workers required. They showed their youthful yearning for romantic adventure in the fabulous plan to send a ship to Asia to return with precious woods and ebony. This was not quite as far-fetched as it sounds: ships had been plying back and forth for centuries between Barcelona or Salou and Egypt, bringing raw cotton for the textiles industry. Gaudí never became involved in the subsequent actual restoration of Poblet, but one of the three friends, Eduard Toda, was later the director of the foundation in charge of the rebuilding of the monastery, which can today be visited in all its restored glory, monks included. This reconstruction of Poblet in the 1890s, along with the monasteries of Ripoll and Montserrat, shows the fervour among conservative Catalan nationalists, feeling the breath of rising anarchism on their necks, to emphasize the nation's Christian roots. Gaudí, Toda and Ribera had played their part in putting Poblet on the map.

The Chaotic City

In September 1868, Gaudí's parents found the resources to send him and his brother Francesc to Barcelona, Antoni for his final year of secondary school and Francesc – the great hope of the family – to study medicine. Here Antoni successfully completed his baccalaureate and, from 1870 to 1873, took additional subjects he needed in order to enter the university to study architecture.

The brothers lived in the overcrowded, sunless slums of the old city in cheap boarding-houses. They moved often, returning to Reus for the long summer holidays. Their first lodging was above a butcher's at Placeta de Montcada 12, beside the great Gothic church of Santa Maria del Mar. In Reus there was nothing like this medieval church, built rapidly by popular subscription and voluntary labour and larger than most cathedrals. It impressed the aspirant architect and inspired his later searches for donations for the Sagrada Família. Other addresses were the *carrer* Cadena, near Les Rambles (Las Ramblas), *carrer* Espaseria 10 and, in 1872, *carrer* Montjuïc de Sant Pere 16.[10] The bustling port city of Barcelona was a more dangerous place than Reus. There was more crime, more political unrest and, most lethally, the cholera epidemic of 1865 and the yellow fever of 1870, which killed thousands of people.

After graduating from his last year of secondary school, Gaudí was scheduled to enter the university's science faculty in 1869 to take the courses he needed for architecture. He delayed starting for a year in a letter that has survived, citing 'political' turmoil as the reason.[11] The following year he did enter, and finally, in October 1874, Antoni Gaudí was admitted to the faculty of architecture at the School of Fine Arts and Trades (Escola d'Arts i Oficis), then located in the Llotja de Mar (medieval Stock Exchange building) in the Pla de Palau. The Llotja, near the beach, had its roots in Barcelona's trading glory in the Middle Ages. Thus Gaudí's first year of architecture study was in a historic building reflecting Barcelona's prestige in both commerce and art. In 1875, architectural studies were transferred to the new School of Architecture (Escola d'Arquitectura) in the University of Barcelona building on the Plaça de la Universitat.

The school was directed by Elies Rogent (1821–1897), a well-known architect who had himself designed the neo-Gothic university building and supervised its construction between 1863 and 1872. An architecture school was something new: before the nineteenth century, buildings had been designed and constructed by master masons, in the main anonymous. By the 1860s and '70s, though, the Industrial Revolution had produced throughout Europe a class of capitalists who wanted distinctive houses to underline their wealth and prestige. The architect controlling a complex building became a professional category separate from the master mason. Schools like the one in Barcelona were opened to train this new and newly respectable profession.

The neo-Gothic university where Gaudí studied.

The master masons' guild did not give up without a fight. Indeed, between 1859, when Barcelona's walls came down, and 1864, very few buildings were actually constructed in the new Eixample (Expansion), the grid-based, inland district of the city. The master masons insisted that they would be the builders, according to their standard building practice. Finally, the architects, backed by the industrial magnates, won out. In Elies Rogent's architecture school, the new generation of architects were taught both the technical side, involving geometry, mathematics and engineering, and the fine arts side. The modern architect is both technician and artist. Gaudí was among the first.

Unlike most students, Gaudí had to work his way through university, which he was able to do in the studios of several School of Architecture teachers. Various names have come down to us: he assisted the architect Francesc de Paula del Villar (1828–1901; whom he was later to replace as the architect of the Sagrada Família) in designing a grotto at the monastery of Montserrat. He also took jobs in the workshops of various artisans, both ironworkers and carpenters. This underlines a distinctive feature of Gaudí during his later decades of fame: he enjoyed skilled manual work and often knew as much as the artisans themselves about transforming glass, iron and wood into parts of buildings.

Among these jobs, he worked for a master builder, Josep Fontserè (1829–1897), in Barcelona's Parc de la Ciutadella and is thought to have made the calculations for the lake and to have assisted in the design of the extravagant cascade overlooking it. The 1868 'Glorious Revolution' that had ousted the monarchy led to the destruction of the hated citadel that had dominated the city since 1714: the new park, bearing the citadel's name and still there today, was laid out in the following years. Robert Hughes is not too far out in his opinion that 'the Cascade, an enormous allegorical fountain . . . is a work of almost unsurpassable ugliness, pomposity, and eclectic confusion.'[12]

Gaudí was also for a time a machinery draughtsman in the Padrós & Borràs workshops. He worked, too, on the design for the Born market, one of the first constructions to use industrially produced ironwork. This was made at La Maquinista, the

Cascade in Ciutadella Park, Barcelona.

metalworks founded by the magnate Joan Güell (of whom more in Chapter Two). Gaudí was learning about the very latest industrial techniques at the same time as he was soaking his mind in Catalonia's medieval history and building styles. At times he was doing several jobs at once. His diary records that in 1876–7 he was working on projects for as many as four of his teachers' architecture studios at the same time. Sometimes over-enthusiastic hagiographers of Gaudí make him responsible for the structures and buildings he worked on as a student. He was not. Gaudí often participated in the design, certainly learned from these established architects, and very probably tried out his own ideas, but he was not responsible for the building. He was a student employed by the architect or builder.

There was no shortage of jobs. After demolition of the city walls and then the breaking of the master masons' monopoly, for the rest of the century the plain – the area now known as the Eixample – became a massive building site. The city that had occupied 20 hectares (50 acres) of the old city now spilled across 200 hectares (500 acres), most of it agricultural land. Builders, artisans and architects were in high demand. This was not specific to Barcelona. Vienna's Ringstrasse and Baron Haussmann's new Paris were being laid out at the same time.

The Awkward Student

In 1873, Gaudí's parents sold their workshop in Reus and came to live in Barcelona to care for the great hopes of the family, their two sons. They expected little from their daughter Rosa, who had married a musician with little money and too much fondness for drink. Disaster struck. Francesc, who was working as a doctor by the end of 1875, died suddenly at the age of 25 in July 1876. Two months later, his and Antoni's grief-stricken mother Antònia died too, aged 63.

This was the darkest year of Gaudí's life. He had lived his exciting first years in the big city with Francesc. Now Antoni was left to care for his elderly father, which he was to do for the thirty remaining years of his father's life. At the time he recorded nothing of his feelings, though in later years he told friends that this was his most anguished period. We have access to Gaudí's diary or notebook for these years, known as the Reus Manuscript. Whereas several hundred pages of writing, plasterwork and drawing were destroyed in the sacking of the Sagrada Família workshop in the July 1936 outbreak of the Spanish Revolution, this notebook survived because Gaudí's successor as the architect of the basilica, Domènec Sugranyes (1878–1938), had donated it to Reus's museum in 1934.[13] Its importance is heightened because, except for one newspaper article in 1881, it is the only writing by Gaudí that survives. Unlike the academics and politicians who were his contemporary architects, Gaudí was not given to composing articles for the press.

The notebook's scant entries run from 1873 to 1879. They indicate the multiple projects he was engaged in as a student-apprentice working his way through college, with several drawings of these projects and his own ideas. They include interesting 'Notes on Ornamentation' and a thousand words of a diary started on 21 November 1876 which lapsed two months later. This includes the entry for 25 November 1876: 'I must work hard to overcome the difficulties.' Most commentators see in this rare personal comment that Gaudí was referring to his brother's and mother's deaths. He flung himself into work to avoid dwelling on his bereavements.

Gaudí took five years to complete his architecture studies and qualify. This was not just due to having to work to support himself and what remained of his family. He was also called up for compulsory military service, joining the infantry reserve in February 1875. Probably through influential contacts in the School of Architecture, he was able to do his military service on a part-time basis while remaining in Barcelona. The 'mili' could mean being posted anywhere in Spain, even to Spanish Morocco, but he managed to avoid this fate. The Third Carlist War lasted until 1876, but Gaudí did not have to fight. The posting allowed him to carry on more or less as normal with his studies and work.

Gaudí was painstakingly slow and thorough; he won a reputation as a difficult, though brilliant, student. He neglected certain aspects of his coursework to spend hours in the library. He was probably not too popular with the librarians as, according to some accounts, he on occasion tore up books so as to carry portions round in his pockets. Certainly, he was an obsessive commentator in margins and marker of passages.

He immersed himself in books on Moorish and Indian architecture. Gaudí was never to visit Asia, and a possible visit to Tangier was the furthest he got into Africa, but the photographs (at that time a new invention) and models of Moorish and Eastern architecture in the school's library made these styles a lifelong influence. Photos meant that Gaudí's generation was the first that could study 'caliphs' palaces . . . Persian towers, Indian stupas, arcaded pavilions and mosques in Cairo' without having to travel.[14]

Apart from his fascination with the photos of faraway buildings, Gaudí gained a solid knowledge of new materials, such as cast iron, steel, panot tiles and reinforced concrete, not just from his jobs but in his classes.[15] He learned how to determine materials' pressure on a building's structure with mathematical accuracy. Master masons would know traditional materials and maths, too, but the school was open to the new inventions. It also emphasized the theory and history of art and architecture, knowledge that distinguished the new architect from the traditional mason.

Gaudí was a student deeply rooted in his own land's traditions – the Catalan vault, brick arches, the Gothic cathedrals and civil buildings – but with huge curiosity for other cultures and styles. Architecture for him was not just putting up a nice-looking building but intimately associated with ideology, the way he wanted society to develop. The stubborn and eccentric student Gaudí educated himself in his own way, running the risk of failing his course. He had no sympathy with the abstract character and neoclassical trend of some of the university courses. He was not all individualist arrogance, though: he was practical enough to design, as part of his coursework, a pavilion for the 1876 Philadelphia Centennial Exhibition in a conventional style. When he had to, Gaudí was able to give his teachers what they wanted.

He also attended philosophy, aesthetics and literature classes, in particular the lectures on the theory and history of art of the

Antoni Gaudí i Cornet, aged 26.

renowned Manuel Milà i Fontanals (1818–1884), who preached against elitism and that art had to be part of daily life. Milà i Fontanals was a philosopher and philologist whose research into languages found, doubtless to Gaudí's delight, that Provençal and Catalan were strong influences on Spanish and not vice versa. Spanish might be the language of the state, spoken by many millions, but Catalan and Provençal preceded it in the development of local languages from Latin.

His end-of-course project was a section for the Paranimf (Main Hall) of the university, which shows already Gaudí's unorthodox combination of different styles (or, a more hostile commentator might say, uncombined patchwork eclecticism). The daring drawing has a circular central space with Moorish-style iron arches, then square walls and neoclassical columns on both sides: an air of lightness in the middle and severity on the outside. He passed, but without distinction: one can venture that this unorthodox mixture of styles confused the university lecturers. Luckily, his teachers, several of whom had employed him, recognized his talents and bent the rules to allow him to submit this special project to a jury.

Elies Rogent is said to have made the famous comment at Gaudí's graduation on 15 March 1878: 'Gentlemen, today we are in the presence of either a genius or a madman.'[16] His friend the sculptor Llorenç Matamala reported that Gaudí told him ironically later that day: 'Llorenç, they tell me I'm an architect now.'

2

Influences

This chapter discusses the Catalonia into which Gaudí was born and the social and political background that moulded his ideas and behaviour. His were times, even more than most, of massive conflict and upheaval. The chapter goes on to look at the diverse influences that formed him as an architect.

Like many other bright young men wanting to rise, the brothers Francesc and Antoni Gaudí moved from a provincial town to their country's capital. A non-Spanish person might think that Madrid was Gaudí's country's capital, but for most young Catalans, then as now, the word *país* (country) is used for Catalonia and its capital is Barcelona, whereas Madrid is the capital of the *estat*, or state.

Lost Glories

Chapter One has commented that Reus was a particularly Catalanist city, with the wound of the confiscation of its canal money still raw in Gaudí's time. He grew up in the main generation of the Catalan Renaixença, which took off as a cultural movement in the early to mid-nineteenth century and then as a political one in the last decades of that century. The great many among this generation who became nationalists were inspired to study the past as an essential step towards the recovery of Catalonia's former glory. The fascination of Gaudí and his friends for Poblet, the burial place of the Counts of Barcelona in the Middle Ages, led them to wider reading and discussion of the past of their country.

They saw it had declined and found it had been defeated and oppressed. The fallen stones made them angry.

They found that the Crown of Aragon, which included Valencia, Aragon and Catalonia in a federation led by the Count of Barcelona, had been the most powerful military and trading state in the western Mediterranean from the thirteenth to fifteenth centuries. Its possessions included Sardinia, the Balearic Islands and Sicily. The Crown of Aragon's empire even reached Greece. For seventy years the four-barred Catalan flag flew on the Acropolis in Athens. 'There is no jewel in the world more beautiful than the Parthenon,' Pere (Peter) 'the Ceremonious', Count of Barcelona (r. 1336–87), averred proudly.

The Iberian Peninsula moved dramatically towards unity in 1469 through the marriage of Ferran of Aragon and Isabel of Castile (Ferdinand II and Isabella I in English). They became joint monarchs of the new country, Spain, in 1492. The state placed its capital at Madrid, in Castile and at the centre of the peninsula. Though Madrid was the geographical centre and now the political capital, Barcelona and Seville remained the economic centres. The shift in influence from the Mediterranean (and Barcelona and Valencia) to the Atlantic (and Cádiz and Seville) after Columbus's arrival in America contributed decisively to the centuries-long political decline of Catalonia. A long story of restrictions, occupation and battles climaxed in the War of Spanish Succession, when the Bourbon forces of Philip V, the former Duc d'Anjou installed on Spain's throne by France, defeated Valencia in 1707 and occupied Barcelona after a year-long siege on 11 September 1714.

The catastrophic defeat of 1714 saw the suppression of the last vestiges of Catalan autonomy. Its government, the Generalitat, founded in the fourteenth century, was removed and direct, military rule from Madrid imposed. Education, justice and government were to be conducted in Castilian Spanish, not Catalan. The university was closed; fortresses were built in Lleida and Barcelona to control these cities.

Gaudí and his Catalan-speaking friends were educated at school in a version of history that denied the past imperial and trading glories of Catalonia. Their schooling and writing were in Spanish, the normal language of official discourse. Gaudí and his friends would have had to plough through history books and discussion to arrive at the reality of Catalonia's history. This they did, but it was only possible because they were part of a social, cultural and intellectual movement, the Renaixença. To repeat, knowledge of this suppressed history made them fervent and angry.

Capital Accumulation

The economic recovery of Catalonia preceded the cultural and political renaissance. Despite the suppression of national rights in 1714, Catalonia's integration into the Spanish state did not halt its economic growth. From the late seventeenth century, so buoyant was trade that there were British consuls at Reus. Just one of several British firms, Heathcot & Crowe, exported about 2.5 million litres (660,000 gal.) of *aiguardent* from Reus to England and Holland between 1690 and 1696. By the later eighteenth century, Catalan commerce was finding new outlets, particularly after Charles III's decree of 1778 that allowed Barcelona to trade with the Spanish Empire in the Americas and the Caribbean. The wealth that poured back into Catalonia from sugar and cotton plantations in Puerto Rico and Cuba, in particular, marked the country. To put it crudely, slave labour in the Caribbean created fortunes that were then invested in Catalonia's Industrial Revolution. All over the region there are big country houses, known as *masies*, each shaded by a tall palm rising by its front door and curling its fronds over the roof. The palm is not indigenous to Catalonia: only the scrubby small palm, the *margalló* or palmetto, whose hearts are served in restaurants, is native. The tall palm tree is the symbol of the successful *indià*, the poor boy who fled poverty as a teenager and returned from the Indies in triumph. Most *indians* did not prosper. They never returned, struck down by tropical diseases, or came back in rags. Several who succeeded are the legendary founders of Catalan business dynasties.

One of the most famous was Joan Güell, born in 1800 in Torredembarra, on the coast just north of Tarragona. It is worth summarizing his life, both because his son was to be decisive in

Gaudí's career and for the background that Güell's extraordinary life gives to the world Gaudí was born into. As a child Joan looked after his family's sheep before, as a teenager, emigrating to Santo Domingo. He came back to study in Barcelona, but his family went bankrupt and he returned to the Americas in 1818, this time to Cuba. He started as a clerk, but his entrepreneurial dynamism led to his gaining control of much of Havana's export trades, based on produce from slave-worked plantations. By 1835 he was a wealthy returnee to Catalonia. After a trip round Europe to inspect other economies, he identified a key weakness of Catalonia's burgeoning textile industry: it had to import its machinery. Back in Barcelona in 1838, with other capitalists and foreign technicians he founded in 1839 La Barcelonesa, which manufactured and repaired heavy machinery for textile plants. Güell also co-founded a textile factory called Güell, Ramis y Compañía, known popularly as the Vapor Nou (New Steam). This used the most modern looms to manufacture hard-wearing corduroy clothing for workers and peasants. In 1855 he founded La Maquinista, the plant in Barceloneta that ended up manufacturing rolling stock for the new railways throughout the Spanish state.[1]

When his friend Josep Sol i Padrís, president of the Catalan Employers' Association and managing director of the Vapor Vell (Old Steam) textile factory, was shot dead on 2 July during the general strike of 1855, Güell and his family retreated to Nîmes, home of denim (*de Nîmes*). Returning to Barcelona, Güell founded a newspaper and became a member of parliament in Madrid to argue the case for Catalan industry. He failed to get Madrid to adopt protectionist measures against competition from England and Holland, though in the years after his death this was achieved.

A number of points can be drawn from Güell's fabulous career. First, a great deal of the money for Catalonia's industrial development came from tobacco, sugar and cotton plantations worked by enslaved people in Spain's American colonies. This was not the only source of investment, for exports of hazelnuts, *aiguardent* and other products were profitable, too. Second, the lack of coal in Catalonia (there was some, but it was of poor quality) meant that profits were narrow. Without a protectionist policy, the new industrialists were driven to hold wages low. This led to the fierce battles in nineteenth-century Catalonia between a new working class and new capitalists. Many of these bosses, like Güell, had been in their youth more accustomed to dealing with enslaved people. The workers came from a long history of banditry in the hills and urban revolt. The two new classes were doomed to clash violently. After the destruction of the Bonaplata *vapor* (steam-driven factory) and killing of the military governor in 1835, four workers were executed. Bosses and supervisors were killed in revolts. In the biggest of these, the Jamància uprising of 1843, workers refused to pay a toll to enter the city, and several died in the ensuing disturbances, finally subdued by the Spanish army's artillery shelling the city from the hill of Montjuïc. The motto of the 1855 first general strike in Barcelona was a stark 'Unions or Death'.

This was the background of violent class struggle that Francesc and Antoni Gaudí found when they arrived in Barcelona in 1869. Though Catalonia's new capitalists relied on the Spanish army to put down working-class revolts, they were also open to the mood of resistance to the state embodied in the Renaixença. The more Catalonia developed industrially, the more distant it was from a Madrid whose economy was not industrial but based on large, inefficient agricultural estates, the military caste and a state bureaucracy. The state's refusal to implement protectionism led many big capitalists to develop nationalist consciousness.

A more immediate impact on the Gaudí brothers on first arrival in the capital was the building boom. From at least the 1830s there had been constant clamour to knock down the walls enclosing the old city. Several interests coincided. Most people lived in overcrowded tenements with rudimentary sewage disposal and the consequent cholera epidemics and endemic tuberculosis. The average age of death among the poor was about thirty. The rich pressed the Madrid government, for they derived no pleasure or health, either, from living amid these slums. And, decisively, industry needed to expand. Already in the 1830s, capitalists had started to have factories built in Sants and Poblenou, outside Barcelona's walls.

Finally, in 1859, the walls came down and Ildefons Cerdà's plan for the Eixample, the Expansion district over the plain, was approved.

By 1869, much of the Eixample was a building site. When the brothers walked into this area they would have seen buildings shooting up all over. Imagine what it meant to urbanize 7 square kilometres (3 sq. mi.) of land in forty or fifty years. The peak years were from 1890 to about 1910, but even in 1869 it was clear to the seventeen-year-old who intended to become an architect that there would be no shortage of work.

Cultural Renaissance

The Catalan cultural renaissance, which in the 1880s developed into political organization, got under way in the 1830s, at much the same time as the Industrial Revolution. The first *vapor*, Bonaplata, started operations in 1833. That very same year, a Catalan clerk working in Madrid, Bonaventura Aribau, published a poem, 'Oda a la pàtria' (Ode to the Fatherland). This was not Aribau's original title; nor was the sentimental poem designed as a call to the rebirth of a nation. But the poem's nostalgia for Catalonia and lament for the loss of its language meant it soon became a cultural call to action.

The Renaixença was a Romantic movement to recover Catalan pride a century after its language and rights had been crushed by the Spanish state following the 1714 sacking of Barcelona. It was part of the nineteenth-century articulation of the idea of 'nation': think of Garibaldi's 1850s campaigns in Italy, constantly in the news during Gaudí's childhood, or the struggle to found a Greek nation, romanticized all over Europe by Byron's participation and influential on Gaudí's generation. While the Industrial Revolution and the fierce class struggle it entailed were the social background, the constant music and tension, to Gaudí's life, and while the accompanying political upheavals moulded his conservative reaction, the Renaixença and Catalan nationalist movement were closest to his heart. The movement led Gaudí to reject most things Spanish and to look for his inspiration to medieval times, when Catalonia had been a powerful nation.

A profitable analogy can be made between Gaudí and his near-contemporary and friend in the 1880s and early 1890s, Catalonia's national poet, Jacint Verdaguer (1845–1902), who like Gaudí was a conservative nationalist with a mystic view of Catalonia's glorious past. Verdaguer was born in the village of Folgueroles, near Vic, to a peasant family. Like many bright sons of poor families, he entered a seminary to gain an education. Like Gaudí, he showed little religious commitment when young. He failed his exams and was rebuked for writing non-religious poetry. Eventually he was ordained in 1870 and developed a serious religious vocation.

At the Vic seminary, Verdaguer moved in circles of young Catalanist intellectuals. They insisted on using Catalan not just in speech, as the urban poor and peasantry had always done, but in writing too. The Renaixença became entwined with *excursionisme*, rambling or mountain walking. In the 1860s, while Gaudí was climbing hills and investigating ancient ruins in southern Catalonia, Verdaguer was doing exactly the same in the Pyrenees of northern Catalonia. The ramblers were nature-lovers, and Verdaguer's great impact as a poet was achieved by combining close observation of nature with Catalanist feeling. Mount Canigó, in 'North Catalonia' (departments of France now, but part of Catalonia before 1659) and the title of one of Verdaguer's most famous poems, was both a symbol of Catalan nationalism and a real, mighty, snow-capped mountain. Verdaguer combined his high-flown Romantic sentiments about Catalonia's glorious past with direct language. He brought vernacular and literary Catalan together. As Arthur Terry wrote in his summary of Catalan literature, Verdaguer had 'a visionary sweep which at the same time is rooted in direct observation'.[2] One could say exactly the same of Gaudí: grandiloquent language and mystic sentiment about a great lost nation alongside concrete, detailed observation of the natural world.

Catalan nationalism had reactionary strands, with strong fundamentalist religious traits. The peasantry, who had conserved the language against persecution, was seen as the backbone of the nation, with the *casa pairal*, the patriarchal house, as its fundament. Priests watched over this traditional structure, inveighing against

Gaudí's friend, the poet Jacint Verdaguer.

the revolutionary ideas beginning to emanate from the new working class in the godless cities. In his scrawly handwriting, Gaudí romanticized the *casa pairal* in his notebook in 1876:

> The house is the small nation of the family. A man's own home is his native country . . . It is impossible to imagine one's own home without family . . . The family home has been given the name casa pairal. On hearing this name, who does not recall some beautiful place in the country or in the city?[3]

It is a poignant passage because of the recent deaths of his brother and mother. It is poignant, too, to read now because Gaudí never fulfilled the dream of creating his own family.

Verdaguer's poems had practical consequences. His powerful 'The Two Bell-Towers', the epilogue to his 1886 epic *Canigó*, lamented the ruinous state of the Pyrenees' Romanesque churches. In a potent mix of religion and nationalism, he called on Catalans to restore their desolate churches and rebuild their oppressed country. The young Gaudí, Toda and Ribera were thinking along the same lines in their plans for Poblet.

In 1871, in his last major act before his death in 1872, the patriarch Joan Güell ensured the continuation of his dynasty, presiding over the wedding of the decade: his son Eusebi married Isabel, daughter of the wealthiest *indià* of his generation, Antonio López. López was to become the patron of Verdaguer. He hired the poet as his private chaplain, in which capacity he travelled all over Spain and Europe with the López family. Verdaguer lived in the López mansion on Barcelona's Rambles. López paid for the publication of his other major epic, *L'Atlàntida*, in 1877. It was a symbol of wealth to have your own priest living in your house, and even more prestigious if that priest was the most famous poet in the land. It also increased hope that you would have support getting into heaven when your life ended, especially if you might be anxious that your fortune was based on slavery.

In his last years, Verdaguer fell into religious obsession, like Gaudí, and disgrace, unlike Gaudí. Both were great artists who became religious fanatics at the end of their lives, although when young they were worldly. Both depended on the patronage of the sons of *indians*: the sons whose rough-and-ready fathers' cash enabled them to lead highly cultured, leisured lives. Money brought Eusebi Güell and Claudio López power and luxury, but it was the art of their employees that brought them immortality.

In short, the principal contexts for Verdaguer's and Gaudí's lives were the rebirth of Catalan language and culture and the growing consciousness that Catalonia was a nation; the first globalization, whereby slave labour in the Americas sparked the Industrial Revolution in Europe; and the workers' struggle against terrible labour and living conditions.

Viollet-le-Duc

The above paragraphs summarize the given political and social background to the young Gaudí studying in 1870s Barcelona. He also, of course, consciously chose his road. The first chapter glimpsed the student Gaudí spending hours in the library pursuing his own interests while neglecting some of his coursework: only some, for he was no fool and learned the necessary basics of architecture, that is, questions of structure, weight and loads. However, he was unenamoured of abstract subjects such as analytical geometry or mechanics. So what was he reading in the library? What were his influences?

Like many brilliant artists starting out, Gaudí was eclectic, a jackdaw plucking what he liked from several traditions. He would find different solutions to architectural challenges in the early years of his career, but dominating them was an Orientalism overlaid on (or integrated into) Gothic shape and stone.

The Gothic influence came from Catalan medieval buildings, which were abundant in Barcelona's old quarter. And it imbued the courses and atmosphere in the architecture faculty of the newly constructed university, itself a neo-Gothic building. In the background stood the dominant figure of European architecture of the time, Eugène Viollet-le-Duc (1814–1879), restorer of Notre-Dame cathedral in Paris and the medieval walled city of Carcassonne. European architecture was at a turning point as the Industrial Revolution toppled old certainties and Romantic nationalism seized young people's minds. It was Viollet-le-Duc who best theorized the break from classical architecture, building by lines and numbers, one might say. His examination of medieval Gothic was immensely influential on Gaudí, who had already envisaged a neo-Gothic restoration at Poblet.[4]

Viollet-le-Duc was no mere imitator of Gothic. He urged the close scrutiny of ancient buildings, not to copy them but to deconstruct them. He studied how they were made in order to improve them with modern techniques. Viollet-le-Duc and Gaudí based themselves on the past so as to then surpass it. In fact, Viollet-le-Duc defended ardently the latest advances in engineering and materials. He compared the skeleton of a Gothic building with nineteenth-century skeletons of iron. Gaudí, too, was in no way averse to the most modern techniques, whether the iron skeleton or frame of the Casa Milà or the cement-based panot tiles he used on the floor of the Torre Bellesguard.

Plaça del Rei. Medieval Gothic square in Barcelona.

Viollet-le-Duc was also instrumental in making architecture a prestigious artistic profession. Gaudí learned an attitude to architecture as well as a theoretical approach. He annotated and underlined his copy of Viollet-le-Duc's manual, *Entretiens sur l'architecture* (1863–72), which contains the famous dictum that 'for an object to be highly beautiful, its shape must have nothing superfluous, but rather the material conditions that make it useful.' This might seem a motto for minimalists, but Viollet-le-Duc (and Gaudí) saw no contradiction between function and adornment. And indeed, in Gaudí's mature work, the beautiful adornment is not slapped on to the structure but is an integral part of it. Some of his later imitators did just add curves and curlicues to ordinary buildings to make them look fancy, but not Gaudí himself.

Juan José Lahuerta, in his close analysis of Gaudí's few writings – that is, the 1878 'Notes on Ornamentation' and the 1881 article – explains how Gaudí sought unity of construction and decoration. In his notes of 1878, Gaudí compared the Parthenon with the 1870s Paris Opera:

[The Parthenon's] rich and beautifully worked materials . . . are not there, he [Gaudí] says, to represent wealth or to 'cover' the building luxuriously; but constitute its essence: the work, down to the smallest detail, is made of these materials.[5]

In contrast, the Opera, built in the 1870s and with its 'marbles from all over the world', is imitative and jumbled. In Lahuerta's view, 'Gaudí is lamenting . . . the material disorder of the building, the confusion between the real and the fake, between rich material and tinsel.'[6]

What is strange is that Gaudí's first great buildings, the Casa Vicens and El Capricho of the early 1880s (see Chapter Four), are precisely a jumble, the mix of styles and materials against which he inveighs in the notes. What is even stranger is that in the Casa Batlló, the Casa Milà and the chapel at Santa Coloma, his great buildings of the first decade of the twentieth century, he achieved this unity of construction and decoration that he had projected as early as 1878, before he had built anything at all.

An anecdote explains, however, that by 1878 Gaudí was already an authoritative and distinguished figure. While still a student, on one of the site trips that Rogent organized, Gaudí went abroad for the first time: to Viollet-le-Duc's reconstruction of the citadel of Carcassonne. According to Josep Ràfols, Gaudí's later collaborator and one of his first biographers, Gaudí was so serious and looked so distinguished that local people took him for the great Viollet himself.[7] This is hardly likely: Viollet-le-Duc was forty years older and spoke French. The point, though, of Ràfols's anecdote was that Gaudí had presence and a powerful personality, even when he was still a student.

Mudéjar and Morris

While Viollet-le-Duc and his interpretation of Gothic were dominant influences, another was the quite distinct Mudéjar style. Mudéjar is the name given to work created by Moorish craftsmen under Christian rule in the twelfth to sixteenth centuries. In Gaudí's early work, minarets, bare brickwork and repetitive motifs with slight variation show the influence of Mudéjar. There was nothing unusual in his interest in Moorish building. Catalonia was part of a Spanish state overflowing with Moorish architecture, though there was little of it in Catalonia itself. The School of Architecture was no hidebound institution but part of a new age, as open to influence from neighbouring France or the Arab world as it was to that of the Catalan past.[8]

Whether Gaudí read William Morris (1834–1896), the British artist central to the Arts and Crafts movement, or the critic John Ruskin (1819–1900) is not clear. However, their ideas were another influence afloat in the air of the architecture school. 'My wish would be to see the profession of the architect united, not with that of the engineer, but of the sculptor,' Ruskin wrote.[9] Machines were 'soulless'. He argued that imperfection in a piece of architecture reflected the artist's pleasure, the joy in his work. Rough edges and surface meant it was not machine-made. Reacting against the ugly industrial age, Ruskin rejected the perfect repetitiveness of machine-made items.

It would be wrong to conclude that Gaudí followed slavishly Ruskin's dictates. Gaudí was a great fan of artisan methods: he commissioned original, sculpted iron pieces and left stone unsmoothed. However, as explained above, he followed Viollet-le-Duc in his use of the most modern materials. Lahuerta attempted to clarify this apparent contradiction:

> In 1878 Gaudí understood that architecture could no longer count on the unique work of great artists; his industrial pedagogy revolves around a realistic question: how to organize production. Clearly, Gaudí was saying no to that mythicised craftsmanship, and also to the banality of standardized mass production, as he makes clear in his article of 1881, and declaring himself in favour of quality industrial manufacturing.[10]

In one sense Gaudí did not reject 'mythicised craftsmanship'. He valued highly the skilled artisans with whom he collaborated. He shared Ruskin's and Morris's rejection of impersonal industrialization, which led them to emphasize the use of materials from the local area and employ traditional artisans to create beauty. Morris thought that artwork should be drawn from nature, be useful as well as beautiful and should also exude spiritual feeling, three ideas close to Gaudí's heart. The influence of Ruskin and Morris on Catalan artists and architects of Gaudí's generation was seen in 'a great revival of decorative ceramics, ironwork and stained glass', all key features of Gaudí's work.[11]

A clear example of how Gaudí combined artisan methods and 'quality industrial manufacturing' is the palmetto-leaf fence at the Casa Vicens. This was moulded from nature – an actual leaf – and then reproduced industrially.

Orientalism

We should round off this chapter on the various influences on Gaudí by mentioning the fashion for Orientalism, very clear in his early work: the Casa Vicens and El Capricho. Robert Hughes summarized how '[the Orient] evoked minarets and domes, fretted vaults, serpentine calligraphy in tile, and water trickling into shallow basins.'[12] Gaudí could not have been ignorant of the work of Reus's other great artist, Marià Fortuny (1838–1874), whose paintings of turbaned Arabs, ruffled tapestries and half-naked women were all the rage throughout 1880s Europe.

Fortuny was the great Spanish painter of Oriental scenes, or scenes that he and Europeans imagined were depictions of Arab countries. These were richly decorated interiors with twisting, hanging drapes, and colourful exteriors with minarets and tiles. In Fortuny's most notorious picture, *The Odalisque* (1861), a naked woman stretches out submissively before her master, dressed in Arab clothing. The emotion is transmitted by crumpled sheets, curtains and clothing, the rumpling giving the fabrics the play of light and shadow. As often, art allowed semi-pornographic subjects that were titillating to men to be seen in public. After Fortuny's death, his paintings sold for huge sums. Unlike Fortuny, Gaudí never visited Arab or Asian countries, but he had studied the models and photographs of those countries' buildings in the School of Architecture library.

Gaudí's early works were contradictory mixes of multiple influences. Art critics like Robert Hughes or Nikolaus Pevsner were often disdainful of his highly personalist eclecticism, sometimes with some reason. The glory of Gaudí's career is that he then integrated these disparate influences into a new, original artistic whole. The jackdaw became a mighty eagle.

3

The Free-Thinking Family

On qualifying as an architect in March 1878, Gaudí had no wish
to continue as an assistant on others' projects. He started looking
for his own commissions. Indeed, he was organizing them before
graduation. He was confident of his abilities as an architect. And
he needed the money, for he had to support his father and his
sister, Rosa. In 1879 further family tragedy struck, bringing Gaudí
still greater responsibility. The unfortunately married Rosa died
at the age of 35, leaving a young daughter whom her husband was
unwilling or unable to look after. At the age of 27 Antoni was the
only survivor of five siblings. For a few years Gaudí sent Rosa's
daughter, also Rosa (often known by the diminutive, Rosita), to
board with nuns at a school in Tarragona. In holidays she lived with
Antoni and his father in Barcelona.

This would be Gaudí's household until the deaths of both
his father and niece in the early twentieth century. Those that
remained of this once sizeable family now opted definitively to
stay in Barcelona. Gaudí sold his sister's house, which had been his
mother's, in Reus.

Early Commissions

Gaudí's first commissions were modest but interesting. The most
flamboyant was the kiosk he was asked to design in May 1878 by an
inventor-businessman, Enric Girossi. Girossi asked the Barcelona
City Council for permission to install around the city twenty public
urinals combined with flower stalls that would be staffed and open

24 hours a day. The council approved. Gaudí designed a fabulous urinal-cum-flower stall, with the modern touch of holes in marble columns to both water the flowers and rinse the urinal. The base was marble; the roof was glass supported by iron, with a canopy to display adverts. Both flowers and the urinals would be bathed in light. Gaudí showed his playfulness, something he never lost even in his melancholic later years, by putting words of Andalusian popular songs and drawings of red carnations on the roof. Alas, Girossi went broke. Gaudí was probably never paid. The urinal-flower stall was never built. Gaudí's first public building, as colourful and imaginative as some of his later great mansions, never got off the drawing board.

This was by no means the only project not to be built: a risk of the profession when you are unknown. Another entrepreneur, Juli Carré, won a concession to place advertising hoardings in Barcelona's streets. Gaudí was hired to design cast-iron and glass hoardings to be lit by gas at night. His project is dated 15 April 1878. Carré, however, never paid the city council for the concession, and the hoardings were never constructed. Despite these failed projects, Gaudí was being paid elsewhere. He was commissioned by a businessman, Pau Miró, to design the railings and roof for a small theatre in his garden at Sant Gervasi, a village just outside Barcelona (now part of the city). Gaudí's notebook records that he made moulds for an older friend, the architect Joan Martorell (1833–1906), in July that year. That same month he assisted on work repairing the roof of the city's cathedral. These were small, routine jobs, but they showed that Gaudí had varied contacts and could earn a living as an architect.

The first commission of his that survives to this day, albeit in a distorted form, dates from that same 1878. The city council had decided to renew its street lighting as part of the hectic modernization of those years of growth after the walls came down in 1859. The architect chosen by the council died suddenly. Martorell used his influence to get the contract for Gaudí. In a letter of 27 February, just before Gaudí's graduation, the mayor commissioned the gas lighting from the 'young and diligent architect'.[1]

These first wholly Gaudí works are lamp posts that can be seen today in the magnificent, porticoed Plaça Reial in the Gothic quarter of Barcelona, a square whose many palms become long and lean as they stretch up towards the light. Gaudí had hoped to have his designs installed throughout the Eixample, but finally only two were put up in the Plaça Reial. These are six-armed; two similar three-armed ones also by Gaudí were installed in nearby Pla de Palau a

Gaudí's earliest surviving commission. Lamp posts in the Plaça Reial, Barcelona.

few years later. A lover always of colour ('Nature is never in greys,' he wrote),[2] Gaudí specified that the lamp posts in the Plaça Reial should be multicoloured. However, they were painted black in an ill-done 1982 restoration. For these lamp posts, Gaudí made a plaster model in the workshop of his friend Eudald Puntí (*c.* 1817–1889). It was his custom to make three-dimensional models of his buildings in preference to two-dimensional drawings.

This earliest surviving commission of Gaudí's shows his love of ornamentation. These are lamp posts to be looked at, works of art, not just functional city furniture. The young Gaudí was no minimalist; he was expansive, confident, creative. In addition, the lamp posts contain symbols, which like ornamentation would run through all Gaudí's work. The very latest technology for the gas lamps was combined with maritime shapes and Mercury's winged helmet, to represent Barcelona's history as a great Mediterranean commercial city. Two serpents twist round the main column, their mouths gaping beneath the lamps.

Gaudí showed a trait in this first (and last) public commission that was to recur in his dealings with the Batlló and Milà families 25 years later. He entered into a long dispute about his fees. He succeeded in getting the city council to pay him more than the original sum. This, however, may well be why he never received another commission from the council. Gaudí was argumentative and very sure of his own worth.

Before and after qualifying as an architect in 1878, he was working in Puntí's Arts and Crafts carpentry and cabinetmaker's workshop at Barcelona's *carrer* Cendra 8. A much older artist-craftsman, Puntí was a key person in Gaudí's early career: they worked together until Puntí's death, aged about seventy, in 1889. Next door, at number 10, was the studio of the sculptor Llorenç Matamala (1856–1927), who also taught Gaudí and became his friend and collaborator for the rest of his life. These two workshops were the central points of his informal apprenticeships in sculpture and manual crafts when he was a student and during the first years of his life as a qualified architect. One could say that, after the destruction of his biological family, he created a new family with his collaborators. Gaudí often quarrelled with clients, but he remained faithful to a few lifelong fellow artists.

Gaudí designed his own work desk at Puntí's workshop. In Van Hensbergen's words:

> The desk . . . presented a cleverly wrought balance between function and form . . . Set against the wood, the young architect applied metal decoration which gathered together a 'topographic kingdom'. Snakes, birds of prey, a squirrel and a lizard, a praying mantis, a cockerel, butterflies and bees swarmed through the trailing ivy and sprigs of bay. This was Gaudí's 'Great Book of Nature' – but domesticated and brought safely indoors.[3]

This desk accompanied Gaudí throughout his life and was burned in the sacking of the Sagrada Família workshop in 1936.

The Glove Cabinet

1878 was also the year of Gaudí's legendary meeting with Eusebi Güell (1846–1918), the fabulously wealthy and highly cultured heir of the rough *indià* Joan Güell. This came about through the commission from a glove merchant, Esteve Comella, who had Gaudí design and Puntí make (with Gaudí's hands-on help) a counter for his shop. Comella then commissioned from Gaudí a showcase to display his products at that year's Exposition Universelle in Paris. The cabinet was carved in oak, with slim cast iron supporting irregularly shaped glass windows (not unlike the urinal, perhaps). The strange shapes were not eccentric for eccentricity's sake but were designed to show off the exhibits to best effect.

Robert Hughes was not respectful about Gaudí's glove cabinet, writing: 'This preposterous object looked like a freestanding tabernacle.'[4] A connoisseur of art, and touched by the winds of the Catalan Renaixença, Güell visited Paris for the exhibition and, out of all the hundreds of exhibits, fell in love with the preposterous object. He asked who had designed this showcase for gloves that was both exotic and practical and was told that its author came from a

Eusebi Güell, 1915.

workshop in Barcelona. On returning home, Güell visited Puntí's workshop and was introduced to the recently qualified architect Gaudí. Despite their differences in origin, class and education, Gaudí and Güell hit it off. They became friends and remained so until Güell's death. Both were conservative Catalan nationalists. Just as Verdaguer had a mystic vision of the rebirth of Catalonia that he expressed in his poetry, and as Eduard Toda devoted energy to restoring Poblet, so Gaudí saw his buildings as part of the recovery of Catalonia's lost past. Güell's view was undoubtedly more worldly and practical, but he financed much of Gaudí's work, famously giving him a free hand to spend as much as he wanted. Catalan *modernisme* was financed by private capital, not by public commissions as is the norm for showy architecture today. The new wealth in Catalonia's Industrial Revolution was striving to build a new country. The

Catalan bourgeoisie, frustrated at not holding political power in Madrid, poured their energy and spare cash into art.

Güell was to become the architect's greatest protector and client. Nevertheless, his patronage did not start at once. He did arrange for his father-in-law, Antonio López, to commission from Gaudí the liturgical furniture (armchair, bench and prie-dieu) for the chapel and family vault attached to his Palacio Sobrellano in Comillas, in Cantabria, on Spain's Bay of Biscay coast. Puntí finished this furniture around 1880. Gaudí's relationship with Puntí was changing: Gaudí had learned from Puntí; now he was bringing work to the carpenter.

Anarchism in Mataró

The other important commission of 1878 implies a controversial relationship of Gaudí with anarchists, and indeed draws Gaudí away for a time from his Christian beliefs. Today he is seen quite correctly as an ultra-religious Catholic who wanted to put a giant cross on the roof of the Casa Milà and dedicated his last decade to the Expiatory Temple of the Holy Family, the Sagrada Família. The mature and late Gaudí abhorred anarchist ideas. In his youth, however, this was not always so, though many commentators find this apparent inconsistency uncomfortable. It is not uncomfortable for us looking back, but it is strange, for Gaudí was associating with the conservative upper class at the same time as he was sympathetic to anarchism.

He met another *reussenc*, or native of Reus, Salvador Pagés, who was a weaver by profession and had returned wealthy from New York to live in Mataró, 30 kilometres (19 mi.) north along the coast from Barcelona. In 1848 the first railway in peninsular Spain had been built between Barcelona and Mataró, which was home to many textile factories. Pagés was an anarchist and general manager of L'Obrera Matronesa, a workers' cooperative or industrial village in Mataró.

However, Pagés was no revolutionary anarcho-syndicalist or bomb-throwing anarchist. The word anarchism covered a wide swathe of leftist activity and views. His ideas were closer to Robert Owen's utopian ideas of the 1830s to improve the conditions of factory workers, including the construction of humane housing. Pagés hoped to resolve the conflict between capital and labour through a workers' cooperative. He had the dream of building workers' houses with gardens and a social club. The Mataró cooperative was reminiscent, too, of the schoolboy plans of Gaudí and his two friends to create an ideal community at Poblet. It presaged, too, Güell's very different workers' village that Gaudí would help build at Santa Coloma de Cervelló.

The cooperative, through Pagés, hired Gaudí for the abovementioned houses and club and to redesign the factory buildings. He also designed its flag: a bee, the classic symbol of cooperative work. And he decorated the cooperative's main hall with anarchist slogans: 'Nothing is more powerful than brotherhood' or 'Comrade! Show solidarity, practise goodness.' One can see that these are progressive mottoes, but equally they could be found on the hoardings outside Christian churches. The houses were never built, but the social club and an industrial workshop roofed with parabolic arches were, though today only the latter and

The toilet (in foreground), chimney and shed of the Mataró Workers' Cooperative.

some toilets survive. The roof is particularly interesting, as here for the first time Gaudí used catenary (the word comes from *cadena*, chain) arches, in this case made from short planks bolted together. Hughes sums up the catenary arch for a layperson: 'A catenary is the parabola-like curve traced by a hanging chain. It has no bending moment in it, only pure tension – as in a suspension bridge – or, used upside down as an arch, pure compression.'[5] He concludes about the Mataró cooperative's catenary technique: 'It was daring and cheap to build, the first of Gaudí's fundamentalist structures.' Gaudí's plans for Mataró were shown at the 1878 Exposition in Paris along with the glove cabinet.

Apart from this original architectural method, there are two other interesting features of the Mataró cooperative project: that Gaudí was sympathetic for a period to an anarchist cooperative and that it led to his meeting Josefa Moreu.

There are well-based rumours that, during the late 1870s and early 1880s, Gaudí took part in anticlerical and anarchist café society. If Gaudí had been a writer, we would know what he thought, but – and this will be common in this book – we have to depend on what others said about him. The Cafè Pelayo, no longer in existence but once located on the corner of Barcelona's *carrer* Pelai and Les Rambles was a city-centre meeting place at that time for a group of anti-Catholic intellectuals. Domènech i Montaner, one of Gaudí's fellow architects, though not a man without malice, spread the story of Gaudí's participation in this group. The Catalan writer Josep Pla reported that the group would, as well as talk and complain as is standard among coffee-bar intellectuals, stand outside churches and verbally abuse the faithful as they came out. Gaudí, reportedly, was one of these.[6] The evidence for Gaudí's presence and participation in the Café Pelayo set is all indirect. Whether true or mischievous gossip, the story certainly fits with what we know of his involvement with the godless Salvador Pagés and Josefa 'Pepeta' Moreu of the Mataró Workers' Cooperative.

Pla believed the stories and wrote that it should not surprise us, as Gaudí was 'indescribably contradictory'.[7] He goes on to argue that Gaudí was no cold fish and, whereas cold fish tend to maintain the same opinions because they do not feel strongly, Gaudí was vital and passionate in all he did. Thus, according to Pla, he could fling himself wholeheartedly into atheism, just as he became later more Catholic than the Pope. Not a bad explanation.

In his appearance and manners, too, Gaudí in his first years as an architect was quite different from the image and reality of his later years. The confident young architect was something of a cigar-smoking dandy who dressed in fashionable top hat, waistcoat and boots and displayed a carefully trimmed beard. He was tall and had reddish hair (though rapidly receding) and blue eyes. These blue eyes cannot be seen in the black-and-white photos of the time, but his gaze is clear. Every contemporary who commented on Gaudí refers to his penetrating gaze: he looked people directly in the face while listening or talking to them.

His eyes had a further characteristic, which may have contributed to the effect of his gaze and which Gaudí believed was useful to him in his work. One eye saw with very high definition at a short distance; his other eye was long-sighted. An oculist prescribed a monocle to balance his sight but, according to the architect Joan Bergós (1894–1974), a friend in Gaudí's last years, he threw it away as he found his particular kind of double vision useful.

The unusual eyes and hypnotic stare became part of his reputation for honesty, talent and dedication to his work. Red hair and blue eyes were not common in Catalonia, and Gaudí cut an unusual and impressive figure. His eyes became part of the legend. Here's an over-the-top tribute from someone who knew Gaudí in the latter's old age:

> I have never seen in anyone's look so much joyous light and gentle humility combined with such a hard, penetrating gleam. His eyes could sear through vanity and empty pomposity like bolts of lightning.[8]

One day, Pagés invited this blue-eyed boy to visit friends of his in Mataró, the Moreu family. They got on well. Gaudí became a frequent visitor at weekends, sometimes arriving hand in hand with his niece Rosita, and was warmly welcomed by this open, liberal, anticlerical family with a son and two daughters. Little else is known about Gaudí's personal life at the time, but one can imagine that life with his father and niece in a Barcelona flat, the rest of the family dead, was not a bundle of fun. Here with the Moreu family he found for a few years, in a house with a garden and bright young women, a welcoming home. They in turn admired his good looks and were touched by his devotion to his niece.

In 1885, after several years of visiting the house, Gaudí asked Pepeta Moreu to marry him. Pepeta was the elder daughter, born in 1858. Curiously, she too had red hair. She was divorced from a short-lived marriage with a wealthy *indià* and had returned to live with her parents. She was modern, lively and good-looking. Scandalously, she liked to swim. She was republican and gave classes in the workers' cooperative. She turned Gaudí down. Castellar-Gassol explains the rejection thus: 'Gaudí was skilful with clay, plaster, stone, glass, wood, iron, brass, with the draughtsman's triangle and set-square, compass and pen, but he was clumsy when it came to picking up a knife and fork.'[9] Clumsy manners apart, it seems obvious that a sophisticated, modern woman of anti-monarchist ideas like Pepeta was unlikely to be attracted to a country boy with conservative opinions like Gaudí (even if it is true that he shouted at the Catholic faithful). This is the general view of their relationship. In addition, Pepeta's younger brother, Josep Maria, wrote later that Gaudí 'took little care of his appearance',[10] though this contradicts most other witnesses who saw Gaudí as a dandy. He had formed friendships with wealthy architects such as Joan Martorell and with the extremely refined Eusebi Güell, so was hardly a country hick. Be as it may, Pepeta rejected him. Within a year she was engaged to another man. Gaudí stopped visiting the house with a garden near the sea in Mataró. He probably never approached another woman (or man) in his life. His clothes changed: coloured, fashionable waistcoats gave way to simple dark blouses and trousers, suitable for the workshop and building site. He sublimated his disappointment in work, as he had done years before when grieving for his brother and mother.

Walking

During this period of visits to the Moreu household, Gaudí joined the Associació Catalanista d'Excursions Científiques (Catalanist Scientific Rambling Association). Gaudí belonged to its management committee from 1879 to 1882, was for a time curator of its archaeological museum and participated actively for ten years, often accompanied on excursions by his father. At the same time as he was in the vanguard of architectural modernity, designing flower stall-urinals or a workers' cooperative's hall, he was spending leisure time as he had done in the 1860s, climbing mountains and surveying the great ruins of Catalonia's past. There was no contradiction. These were 'scientific' excursions, not just to walk but to investigate, to learn about this lost nation. Gaudí's nationalism, like that of much of his generation, was rooted in exalting past glories. At the same time, the best way to reconstruct the past was not to copy slavishly the past but to draw on it to build a modern country. He was familiar with the famous conundrum of Viollet-le-Duc: that restoration of a building involved re-establishing it with a degree of integrity that it may never have had. One of Gaudí's great masters was telling him, with subtle recognition of the creativity of restoration, that mere copying is sterile: interpret in your own way.

The Rambling Association also campaigned to prevent the destruction of ancient monuments and organized numerous trips to discover, document and sightsee. As populations grew (that of Barcelona raced from 121,815 in the 1842 census to 504,396 in 1897 – a fourfold rise), cities expanded and demolition destroyed the past. In 1882, Gaudí travelled with another, rival rambling group to Perpinyà (Perpignan), Elna (Elne) and Toulouse. It was his second visit to France, though for Gaudí and his fellow Catalanists this part of southern France was not a foreign country, but North Catalonia, where Catalan was still spoken among a peasantry resistant to the French state's hyper-centralization.

During his period working on the Mataró cooperative's buildings, Gaudí took on other commissions. Two in particular show that he continued in favour with Eusebi Güell. Indeed, some commentators say that Gaudí often attended Güell's intellectual soirées, where Ruskin and Morris were discussed and Dante Gabriel Rossetti and the Pre-Raphaelites were exalted for their return to the purity of medieval forms and their love of rich ornamentation. It may seem surprising to us that such British poets and painters were taken up by these Catalan industrialists and artists discussing energetically how to build a new country. The answer lies in that both Pre-Raphaelites and Catalan nationalists were inspired by medieval glories.

In 1882 Gaudí was involved in two projects, one for Antonio López, Güell's father-in-law, and one for Güell himself. He designed a hunting lodge (never built) for Güell's estate at Garraf, on the coast south of Barcelona. Its project combined brick and stone, like the Casa Vicens and El Capricho, his major buildings started in the following year. The lodge, in Hughes's excited words,

> was to be a fantastically crenellated affair, Oriental-medieval, its main motif an octagonal tower that mingled the towers of the Royal Gate at Poblet with a touch of Hindu stupa. The walls were rustic freestone inlaid with panels, stripes, and checkers of colored tile.[11]

López had earlier commissioned religious furniture from Gaudí and Puntí. He then asked Gaudí to design and construct a pergola for his garden to honour a coming visit by the royal family. It recalls the now long-gone theatre for the garden of Pau Miró that he had designed a few years previously. Shaped like a turban, constructed of iron, with glass balls that shone at dusk and bells of glass that chimed in the wind, the pergola was shipped by train to Comillas. Apparently a workman's head accidentally broke the glass dining table. He was unhurt and Gaudí was said to have made one of his famous remarks: 'Good. We can always make a new table, but not a new workman.' The anecdote is designed to show how Gaudí was unfazed by the needs and wants of the royal family. It confirmed his legend of being independent of the powerful and of being close to his craftsmen. And there is no need to think this was not the case. The glass table was replaced rapidly by a wooden one before the king and his entourage arrived.[12]

The Expiatory Temple

During this period of his visits to the Mataró atheists, Gaudí also received what would become his most famous commission: the Sagrada Família. The project for such a temple of expiation dated back to 1861, when the owner of a religious bookshop in Barcelona's *carrer* Princesa, Josep Maria Bocabella, made a pilgrimage to Rome. Impressed and obsessed by the figure of Joseph, the saint and husband of the Virgin Mary, Bocabella founded the 'Spiritual Association of the Worshippers of Saint Joseph' in 1866. The association acquired tens of thousands of members in the following years. Its success was due greatly to Catholic terror at the ousting of Queen Isabella II in 1868 and the short-lived First Republic of 1873. The association's aim was 'through the intercession of Saint Joseph to achieve the triumph of the Church in the difficult and hazardous circumstances of the world in general and, in particular, our Catholic Spain'.[13]

Bocabella and the association decided to build a temple dedicated to the Holy Family. They collected some 150,000 pesetas from donations during the 1870s and bought a large plot in the village of Sant Martí dels Provençals, in walking distance from Barcelona. These Catalan Catholics were by no means alone. In Paris at the same time, plans were being made to construct the Sacré-Coeur basilica on the hill of rebellious Montmartre, with the aim of expiating the sins of the Communards in 1871. The Church took advantage of the widespread and well-founded fear of revolution among the upper class and a growing middle class. As in Paris, the idea was to build an offering to the glory of God to expiate the sins of Barcelona. These sins were not, of course, committed by the city's *barbarians* – that is, its slave traders and industrial magnates – but rather by the godless workers. From the start, the Sagrada Família basilica was an ideological counter-attack on revolutionary Barcelona.

At 5 p.m. on 19 March 1882, with a large crowd present, including Gaudí, the first stone of the Expiatory Temple was laid on the association's plot. It was to be a Gothic basilica. One of the architecture school teachers for whom he had worked, the elderly Francesc de Paula Villar, was the temple's first architect. However, a year later, Villar resigned because of disagreements with Joan Martorell, who was an adviser to Bocabella. Martorell himself was offered the job; he refused and recommended his friend and protégé Gaudí. The somewhat magical story is that a relative of Bocabella had had a vision that the architect of the temple would have blue eyes. On being presented to the association, Gaudí, aged only 31, got the job. Josep Pla both relates with relish and disbelieves the story of the blue eyes, but poses the question: what other explanation could there be for giving the job to an unknown architect who was working for an anarchist cooperative?[14] No one knows, but Gaudí had already been contracted through the influence of Güell for his first major civil commissions, the Casa Vicens in Gràcia and El Capricho in Comillas on the Cantabrian coast. Martorell, perhaps Güell and the handsome architect's blue eyes were all factors in Gaudí becoming the architect of the Sagrada Família on 3 November 1883, a post he would hold until his death nearly 43 years later.

4

The First Great Houses

Since collections from the devout were the only source of finance for the Sagrada Família, work went ahead piecemeal. In 1886, Gaudí thought that, with 360,000 pesetas yearly, the temple could be finished in ten years. He vastly overestimated the rate of donations.

Very early on, Gaudí worked out where he was heading on this extraordinarily complex project. Not without cunning despite his obsessiveness, and quite soon realizing that it could not be finished in ten years, he persuaded the construction board to build vertically, not horizontally. This would mean that the Nativity facade with its spires, once completed, could be seen from anywhere in Barcelona. Thus, the basilica's construction would remain in the public eye. And this is what has happened. Gaudí explained:

> As this Temple cannot be raised in one generation, let's leave such a clear example of our presence that the generations to come are stimulated to build further bits . . . We have built one complete facade of the Temple so that its importance makes it impossible not to go on with the work.[1]

The temple was to have five naves, a transept, three main outside facades and eighteen spires, making it bigger and higher than St Peter's in Rome. Gaudí conceived the temple as a Bible in stone, narrating the history and mysteries of faith. The towers symbolize Jesus, the Virgin, the Twelve Apostles and the Four Evangelists; the facades evoke the three key moments in the life of Jesus: Nativity, Passion and Resurrection.

The first part to be completed (by 1891) was the crypt, measuring 40 × 30 metres (130 × 100 ft). Gaudí had windows opened in the vault to let in light and air. Unlike the rest of the temple, the crypt is in a recognizably classical style, built in stone, the opposite of the towers' pinnacles of cement and broken glass. After the crypt it was the Nativity facade, constructed during the 1890s, that took priority over the interiors. At the start of his Sagrada Família work, Gaudí would turn up only occasionally and give orders to the builders without taking off his gloves or even getting out of his horse-drawn trap. This suggests that, in the early 1880s, Gaudí was more interested in the chance of earning money and renown from his civil contracts, the great houses that were to make his name over the next 25 years, than in this religious commission.

The year 1883 was Gaudí's breakthrough, as he started work on his first two commissions for houses, the Casa Vicens in Gràcia, then an independent town and since 1897 a part of Barcelona, and El Capricho at Comillas. The rest of this chapter focuses on these two houses, followed by Eusebi Güell's stables and gate to the Finca Güell at Pedralbes, and finally Güell's monstrous townhouse, the Palau Güell, started in 1885.

The most fashionable, wide and expensive street in Barcelona is the Passeig de Gràcia, which runs 1.3 kilometres (nearly a mile) from the old city of Barcelona to the former village of Gràcia. On this broad avenue, now dominated by luxury-brand shops, Gaudí was responsible for two great houses in the first decade of the twentieth century, the Casa Milà and the Casa Batlló, which stand alongside a number of other *modernista* buildings. This style, *modernisme* or Catalan art nouveau (see Chapter Six), dominated during the frenetic building boom of the last decades of the nineteenth century and the first years of the twentieth, when the agricultural land between the Old City and Gràcia was built up, in line with Ildefons Cerdà's grid design for the Eixample (Expansion).

The Casa Vicens

Gaudí's first house, however, was not on the Passeig de Gràcia but further inland, on the outskirts of Gràcia itself.[2] His client was Manuel Vicens, who is usually cited as a ceramics manufacturer. That was another Vicens. Gaudí's Manuel Vicens was a speculator who had made a fortune in the stock market fever that assailed Barcelona in the 1870s. Vicens had first contacted Gaudí shortly after the latter's graduation, but work did not start for a further five years. Vicens wanted to build a home for his small family – he, his wife and an adopted daughter – on a site he had inherited, today the *carrer* Carolines 24–26.

'When I first went to measure the site,' Gaudí reminisced later to Bergós, 'it was completely covered by yellow flowers, which led me to adopt them as a decorative theme in the tiles.'[3] These were yellow marigolds on a green background that alternated with bare white tiles. The dwarf palm tree (*margalló*) that Gaudí also found on this first visit led to the famous palm leaf design on the cast-iron railings between the garden and street. Though architecture inevitably crushes nature under its bricks, Gaudí was passionate to integrate nature into his buildings. And from nature's colourful, extravagantly shaped flowers came Gaudí's propensities for colour and the rococo.

The idea was Gaudí's, but it was Llorenç Matamala who sculpted in clay the palm leaf and Joan Oñós who mass-produced the

Casa Vicens. The 'outside room'.

sculpture in wrought iron. Another trusted colleague, Hermenegild Miralles, did the completely original and exquisite papier-mâché on the roof of the smoking-room. Without these and other skilled craftsmen, Gaudí's ideas could not have been made material.

The Casa Vicens has a magnificent south-facing *tribuna*, the protruding main gallery above the front door common in grand houses of the time, that gives on to what was then a huge garden. Gaudí's childhood and adolescence in the country underlay his inspiration in nature as an adult architect. One of the original features of the Casa Vicens is his creation of what Barcelona architect David Mackay called 'outside rooms', spaces in transit between garden and house.[4] The gallery had wooden, horizontally pivoted shutters to allow in or keep out the heat according to the season. To add to the effect, Gaudí used decoration with birds and flowers on the inside. Recessed walls mean that the window lies behind the outside wall, allowing space for plants to create a microclimate. Coolness was also created by three sources of moving water in the garden: a conventional fountain, a small circular fountain and a huge cascade.

Painted on the plaster of the wide inside lintel of the *tribuna* are flamingos and, as if tossed in the wind, upside-down woodpeckers, starlings and jays and flying leaves. Fully inside this main gallery, red and green dashes of colour imply flowers and leaves. Vegetation runs riot throughout the house's decoration. The house's styles are a whirl of distinct influences. The shutters are of Japanese inspiration; the pleasure in the sound and movement of water, Arabic; the paintings and tiles, Arts and Crafts movement. The most obvious style is *mudéjar*, the term mentioned earlier for the work of Muslim craftsmen under Christian rule. The house's main *mudéjar* features are its multicoloured walls of brick and pressed rubble, covered intermittently with decorated tiles, rising to turrets with very slim supports and coloured glass at each corner.

The three-storey house had three sides, too, as it was placed at the back of the site against the wall of a convent. This position made the garden bigger and the house look larger. Unlike Gaudí's later works, it is still a squarish house, conventional in its structure,

Casa Vicens. Birds everywhere.

though Gaudí was already rounding its square corners and breaking up flat walls with recesses and protrusions. The touches of *mudéjar* in the small turrets, in the shapes of the tall windows and in the bare brick combine with Spanish-style iron grilles on the ground-floor windows. Nikolaus Pevsner (a reluctant admirer of Gaudí's boldness, but no fan) was repulsed, finding it 'a nightmarish farrago of Moorish and Gothic elements'.[5] Pevsner did not believe that the multiple styles cohered into beauty or unity. He is surely right about the unity of styles but fails to respond to the verve, pleasure and daring of the house.

The exterior is striking enough, but it is inside the Casa Vicens that Gaudí's Orientalist imagination really took flight. The house is an explosion of the architect's imagination. No wall or ceiling is bare; everything is decorated. Painted birds and ivy clamber above the flamingos. Plaster carnations and mouldings of hanging branches and fruit twist between the multicoloured beams. Gaudí designed everything: he was an interior decorator, not just an architect of bricks, tiles and mortar. He and his team painted, sculpted and adorned the ceilings and built the furniture: Gaudí was already the 'total architect' he would become famous for in the Batlló and Milà houses. Here, in the Casa Vicens, the styles are overloaded. Everything is crammed in, higgledy-piggledy. 'Ornamentation is everywhere in riotous and tasteless profusion,' as Van Hensbergen put it.[6]

The triumphant glories are the *trompe l'oeil* ceiling in the 'women's room' on the second floor, which looks as if it is open to the sky because of its painted birds and branches that overhang the wall, and the smoking-room below it, with a small door leading into the garden. The latter room is the 'den' where the man could, in the inflamed imagination at least, smoke opium and read decadent literature. 'This corner lifted from the Thousand-and-one nights' is pure fantasy of the Orient.[7]

What you see today in the Casa Vicens is different from the original. In 1925 the house was extended by an architect called Joan Baptista Serra (1888–1962), with Gaudí's blessing. Serra copied Gaudí with care, though different colourings can be seen in

The cascade from the Casa Vicens, reconstructed at Cornellà.

his work. The house is now twice as big as it was in Gaudí's time, though the garden has been lost to the road and neighbouring housing. Some of the railings were removed and are now at the Park Güell. The cascade, which sheltered the house from prying eyes and brought summer freshness with its curtain of water, was knocked down in 1945, victim of post-Civil War building development.[8] Apart from these changes, the house has been restored and refurbished to how it was when Gaudí delivered it to Manuel Vicens.

Rumour and prejudice about the house were rife. Remember that no building as exotic had been seen before. Such a strange house must be inhabited by weird people. It acquired a dark legend after a girl fell from the cascade's steps in 1895 and was drowned in the pool below; in the same year, Vicens died and his widow sold the house. It was also said that the house nearly bankrupted Vicens, as Gaudí's custom of adapting his ideas as the building advanced was costly. The latter is true, but this extra expense has to be weighed against his use of cheap, recycled materials and local stone whenever possible. There seems little basis to the claim of the Vicens's near-bankruptcy, as Gaudí was a friend of the family and often visited them in their country house at Alella in the hills 18 kilometres (11 mi.) north of Barcelona, both before and after the construction of the house in Gràcia.

The Playboy's Whim

The commission for Gaudí's other 1883 house was from the *indià* brother-in-law of Antonio López, Máximo Díaz de Quijano, a playboy looking for a fancy, free-standing house in a forest. Like the Casa Vicens, it is a relatively small house by the standards of Gaudí's later production, though large enough by most people's standards. Recognizably similar in its Orientalist style to the Casa Vicens, El Capricho (The Whim) is different in several ways. Two basic material differences were that this was a house for a single man, not a family, and that Gaudí himself was not present during the construction.

This is one of the few Gaudí buildings outside Catalonia. The new railway network made it possible for the rich, including the Spanish royal family, to escape the heat of Madrid in summer. San Sebastián and Santander (connected to Madrid by rail in 1866) became fashionable spots on the northern coast, green all year round unlike central Spain's high plateau. Comillas, a village on the Cantabrian coast 50 kilometres (30 mi.) from Santander, became extremely fashionable because King Alfonso XII stayed there, invited by López, who was then duly ennobled as Marquess of Comillas. This village was the site for the *Capricho*. The rail journey to Santander was possible from Barcelona, but not simple. Though

Gaudí travelled to Comillas at least once, he is thought never to have met Díaz de Quijano. He entrusted the bulk of the work to Cristòfol Cascante (1851–1889), a friend and contemporary of Gaudí's at the Barcelona School of Architecture who had settled permanently in Comillas to work for López and his colony of rich friends. Bergós alleged that Gaudí told him, many years later: 'Quijano . . . Quijote, I said to myself. Better not go there, as we might well not get on.'[9] Bergós's much later comment may well be designed to excuse the capricious frivolity of Gaudí's building, for surely Díaz de Quijano and Gaudí were equally quixotic in their fantasy.

Though Cascante and Gaudí were in continuous contact by letter, Gaudí's absence makes El Capricho unique in his work. In nearly all his later buildings, he was almost always on site, which meant constant changes and improvisations as problems arose. Perhaps because of his absence, El Capricho was finished in a relatively rapid two years. Díaz de Quijano's whim is a brick and ceramic building with a disproportionately large tower. El Capricho is Orientalist even more vividly than the Casa Vicens. It is no surprise that the bachelor playboy Díaz de Quijano, a music- and plant-loving *indià*, opted for such a house, with its undercurrents of luxury and sensuality forbidden to Catholics. What is surprising is to find so exotic a building in a Spanish provincial town, until one realizes that it was fashionably in tune with the Orientalism that was all the rage in 1880s Europe.

The *Capricho* at Comillas lives up to its name. Of all Gaudí's buildings it is the least functional, not even particularly suitable for its owner. Its most striking feature is the tower of fantasy above the porch of the main entrance, an imitation of a Persian prayer tower. The tower flows heavenwards from the fat, stubby pillars around the porch to the cylindrical, straight-tiled main section with slim windows and then to the platform and roof that, in Rainer Zerbst's words, 'seems to have been freed from any gravitational force', an effect created by the delicacy of the four slender metal pillars supporting the roof.[10] Inside the tower, a corkscrew staircase leads to the small circular platform overlooking the forest, protected by a Chinese balustrade. The tower is decorated with green and

Fantasy in the forest: El Capricho at Comillas.

yellow tiles, picked up by the lines of protruding sunflowers on
glazed tiles between the layers of green ribbing on the round
facades of the building. These outer walls have alternating red and
yellow bricks. Originally the roof consisted of green glazed tiles,
but these disappeared in 1916, replaced by fibre-cement sheets.
The *Capricho* can look a forbidding house in the woods on a misty
day, with the touches of neo-Gothic severity in its brickwork, but
it is transformed in sunlight, when its shining coloured tiles, the
cylindrical tower and the bare brick exude sensuous luxury. It is an
eclectic, joyful building, its colours reflected in the trees, flowers and
red earth surrounding it, and, at the same time, quite alien to its
surroundings, 'like a strange object from another world'.[11]

A 'caprice' is not just a rich man's whim but also a musical
piece, a free and fanciful fragment. The musical theme is picked
up explicitly in the front wall, which has five hollows with sash
windows, whose counterweights on the balconies are metal tubes
that play musical notes when the window is opened or closed.
One window has stained-glass images of a dragonfly and a bird

strumming guitars. David Mackay quoted Byron's affirmation that 'the perfection of architecture is frozen music';[12] Schiller and Goethe talked of the same: perfect beauty resides in live music, but it can be made permanent in a great building. This idea of the Romantic movement at the start of the nineteenth century was still alive late in that century, frozen in Díaz de Quijano's *Capricho* in the forest.

Finca Güell

In 1883, as well as undertaking the Casa Vicens and El Capricho, Gaudí was employed by Eusebi Güell on a major undertaking. In September that year, Güell bought various plots of land around one of his Barcelona houses and French-style garden, to form an estate measuring 30,000 square metres (7 1/2 acres). This spanned today's Avinguda Diagonal, which stretches from the Palau Reial de Pedralbes (Royal Palace of Pedralbes) to the Les Corts cemetery. Güell wanted Gaudí to work on the stables and gate of the new estate. In 1882, Gaudí had designed a lodge for Güell's hunting property in the Garraf hills south of Barcelona, but this Orientalist building never left the drawing board. It was with the Finca Güell (or Güell Pavilions) that the collaboration of Gaudí with Güell was sealed. Gaudí became the Güell family's architect.

The Casa Vicens, the Finca Güell and the Sagrada Família were being built at the same time. Gaudí began to pull around him now a team of collaborators, some of whom would accompany him for thirty years. The most important of these was Francesc Berenguer, son of the head of his primary school in Reus. Though only seventeen years old in 1883 and in his first year at the School of Architecture, he abandoned his course to work for Gaudí. He became Gaudí's intimate friend and right-hand man, working as master builder, on-site boss and accountant. Later he designed several buildings himself, which other architects, including Gaudí, signed for, as he had never qualified. The ironworker Joan Oñós was another long-term collaborator. Gaudí had known Oñós from his student days; the latter's artistry was responsible for all the ironwork discussed in this chapter, so essential to the quality of the buildings. Joan Bassegoda (1930–2012), architect and holder of the Chair in Gaudí Studies (Càtedra Gaudí) from 1968–2000, tells that when Gaudí visited Oñós's workshop at *carrer* Nàpols 278, just a couple of blocks away from the Sagrada Família, Oñós used to make himself scarce, leaving his skilled workers Lluís and Josep Badia to deal with the architect, as Gaudí was always loaded with alterations, new ideas and fresh work.[13] After Oñós's retirement, Gaudí continued to use his workshop, run now by the Badia brothers.

Earlier chapters have explained Güell's admiration for Gaudí's work. Both were Catalan nationalists and shared a view of the role of architecture in the recovery of Catalonia's former glory. It should be noted, too, that the Güell family hailed from Torredembarra, on the coast not far from Reus: they and Gaudí shared roots in that southern part of Catalonia. In addition, their strong egos coincided, rather than clashed: Güell wanted the fanciest and greatest buildings in Spain to be his, and Gaudí wanted his name to live down the centuries in brick, tile and stone. Gaudí's attention to the Mataró cooperative, with its implication of atheism and a gentle brand of anarchism, does not seem to have bothered Güell. Throughout that period, they both took part in the Associació d'Excursions, devoted to recovery, preservation and repair of the past as well as to conversation while walking in the fresh air.

The Finca Güell was Gaudí's first fully fledged work in which Catalanist symbolism was embedded. The symbolism is based on Verdaguer's poem *L'Atlàntida*. It is not known when Gaudí met Verdaguer. There is a record of an excursion to Poblet in May 1882 from Tarragona with a number of artists and priests.[14] This excursion is unlikely to be the first time that the two met, because on this occasion Gaudí and Verdaguer collaborated on an impressive *son et lumière* among the monastery's ruins, of which Van Hensbergen writes:

Nothing could give a more authentic flavour of the cultural matrix that Gaudí was about to enter: a cocktail of Catholicism, romanticism, fraternity, Catalanism, all mixed up with the romantic love of ruins and lost causes.[15]

In his design of the famous dragon gate leading to the stables of the Finca Güell, Gaudí embedded a number of symbols centred on *L'Atlàntida*. Verdaguer's epic poem was inspired by his trips across the Atlantic and was the winner at the 1877 *Jocs florals*, literally 'Floral Games', Catalonia's medieval poetry contest restored in 1859. The famous poem was dedicated to Isabel López, daughter of Verdaguer's patron Antonio López and wife of Eusebi Güell. It was logical that Güell was keen for Gaudí to reflect the poem in his architectural work.

In the poem, Hercules, legendary founder of Barcelona, has to cross the Atlantic to find the Garden of the Hesperides, on the edge of the world. There, in his eleventh labour, the hero kills the dragon Ladon that guards the garden and seizes the prize of the tree that bears golden oranges. The Finca Güell's entrance gate shows the magnificent cast-iron dragon; the pillar beside the gate, the tree with golden fruit. Both Gaudí and Verdaguer were flattering Güell's father and López, who like Hercules had risked all on the dangerous, further edges of the Atlantic and had returned to Catalonia with fabulous wealth, 'golden oranges' and prestige.

The dragon is 'not just heraldic decor but sculpture'.[16] It is a live, real-looking dragon in three dimensions, with wide-open, tooth-filled jaws waiting to bite you, reminiscent of Gaudí's open-mouthed snakes climbing the Plaça Reial lamp posts. When the gate opens, the dragon's iron claw, with four toes like scythes, is raised with threatening realism. Gaudí the architect understood sculpture: remember that he had often seen iron beaten into curves and twisted forms in his family's forges. The dragon gate was constructed at roughly the same time as the palm fence of the Casa Vicens. The former threatens while the latter is peaceful, but they both express emotion through iron. As Pevsner put it, 'So he grew up acquainted with metals, and it is not surprising that the savagery of his ornamental invention appeared first in metal railings and gates.'[17]

Juan José Lahuerta notes that 'this awesome dragon is more than a sculpture . . . It is an essential part of the structure of the gate.'[18] It is a fine example of how Gaudí did not slap on decoration like

Finca Güell. Dragon gate.

paint on a wall but integrated function and adornment. Lahuerta also comments that the dragon sculpture's component parts are industrial: a spring, fine wire mesh, prefabricated chains and 'jaws and fangs . . . of sheet metal'.[19]

Gaudí was also asked to replace the French classical garden. He introduced a number of Mediterranean trees: cypresses, palms and pines. The garden survives in bits. Two works by Gaudí, a simple iron gazebo and one of two fountains, the Fountain of Hercules, still stand in bamboo thickets just in front of the Royal Palace of Pedralbes. One of the pleasures of such 'minor' Gaudí pieces is that no one else is there. You escape the queues (and steep entrance fees) of the Casa Batlló or Sagrada Família. Whereas the dragon on the gate is ferocious, the long, thin reptile through which the water spouts on the Fountain of Hercules is rather benevolent. Its iron claws end not in scythes but in gently rounded toes, and a smile can be detected in the elongated face and beady eyes. Under the bust of Hercules, the fountain shows the coat of arms of Catalonia. Like Güell, Gaudí declared his Catalanism in the Finca Güell, though not yet Catholicism.

The guardhouse by the dragon gate has two floors, with rooms that have a vaulted ceiling with a hyperbolic section that supports ventilation chimneys with coloured tiles. Gaudí adored rooftop ornamentation. Here the relatively plain brick of a small guardhouse is made exciting and exotic by the Arabic-style chimney.

Fountain of Hercules. Friendly dragon.

The stables, to the right of the gate, are where Gaudí used *trencadís* and hyperboloid vaults for the first time.[20] *Trencadís* is the style of decoration created by smashing pottery and glass and setting the broken pieces in mortar. Pieces from curved pots are particularly useful for covering the rounded edges characteristic of Gaudí's buildings. Catenary arches, as in the project for the Mataró cooperative, expand space and increase light. The stables are a functional, working building and, as such, more austere than El Capricho and the Casa Vicens, though Gaudí's 'austere' was more fanciful than most architects' 'frivolous'.

Heavy Metal: Palau Güell

Metal, the sculpted wrought iron so impressive in the Casa Vicens fence and the Finca Güell gate, was dominant on the street facade of the Palau Güell, the building that first made Gaudí famous in Catalonia. In the mansion's huge, rounded twin doors like hooded eyes and in the bars twisted across its windows, the metal is thick, heavy and as threatening as the dragon of the Finca Güell. The two arched doors are filled with decorative iron and between them a standard clings to the wall like a beast from hell.[21] The ironwork twists round itself; the bars fold over the crossbars in molten flaps. Above the doors is a tribune with a row of vertical windows, with two patterns of ironwork alternating.

The ironworker was once again Joan Oñós. There is an anecdote that shows the relationship of Güell and Gaudí, founded on the former's forbearance. When Oñós was fixing the shield of Catalonia to the front wall, a passer-by exclaimed: 'My God, how ugly!' The irascible Gaudí took exception, but Güell showed how to calm Gaudí, commenting: 'Now I like it even more.'

The Palau Güell is one of few *modernista* houses in the Old City of Barcelona. The other main ones are Domènech's Palau de la Música Catalana (Palace of Music) and the café Els Quatre Gats. The Hotel Europa on *carrer* Sant Pau, the London Bar on Nou de la Rambla and the Escribà cake shop on Les Rambles are decorated in a *modernista* style, but Barcelona's *modernisme* is basically a

Palau Güell. Ironwork detail.

feature of the Eixample, as it was there, across the inland plain, that
wealthy industrialists had their houses built in the decades after
the demolition of the city walls. The area near the docks around
the Palau Güell was rough: slum dwellings, sailors on shore leave,
absinthe bars, rubbish in the streets, women selling sexual services
in the doorways. Surprisingly (or not), 140 years later the area is little
changed. It is not clear quite why Güell, the richest man in Spain,

wanted to build in the middle of a slum. Probable factors are that his parents' house was nearby and this old quarter was dotted with magnificent mansions, whether the López family's Palau Moja on Les Rambles or the late medieval buildings across Les Rambles, around the *carrer* Montcada in the Ribera district. Güell wanted the biggest and best, as always, and here he achieved the best, if not quite the biggest, as the site measured only 18 × 22 metres (59 × 72 ft).

The mansion's severity is the result of its design as a rich man's palace in the medieval sense: the wrought iron screams at the poor who surround it, 'Keep out!' In his book *The Essence of Catalonia* (1988), Alastair Boyd associated such a fortress with Güell's later workers' village at Santa Coloma, both examples of 'industrial feudalism': 'This brilliantly executed but frankly sinister building is an extraordinary statement of the architect's view of the industrial magnate.'[22]

The inside contains a magnificent surprise. The 'frankly sinister' iron-clad building on a narrow, dirty street explodes on the first floor into a huge palatial hall soaring towards the light. The straight lines and fortress style melt into splendorous, light-flooded, curving refinement, with numerous limestone columns. Unlike Gaudí's later Casa Milà or Casa Batlló, whose interiors entirely reflect the exterior, the Palau Güell's medieval facade and entrance conceal the modern luxury of the magnate. The palace thus becomes both a forbidding public statement of Güell's wealth, imposing itself on the city centre, and a private lair of luxury hidden from the masses. As well as being transformed from the exterior wall to the interior space, the palace rises from the dark cellar and street below to 'the festival of colour at the top culminating in the golden sunlight of wealth'.[23] Heavy starkness rises to light and grace.

Mackay wrote of this mansion:

Analysis of the structure shows Gaudí to be a master in deploying the arch and the vault, somewhat brutal with his steelwork and frankly unsound as to the stable limits of load-bearing walls, subjected here to stresses that run very closely the risk of buckling.[24]

I took this as a severe criticism of the young Gaudí. As I had read this nowhere else, I asked Carolina García Estévez, Professor of the History of Architecture at the Barcelona School of Architecture, whether Mackay was right. 'Yes, but I take it as praise,' she replied. 'Gaudí was pushing structure to the limits, and the building hasn't buckled, has it?' But why take risks? Why push a structure to the limits? 'Because so daring a building takes your breath away. It extends the possibilities of architecture.'[25] Such a building is what James Joyce's *Ulysses* is to the conventional novel.

The *palau* was commissioned in 1885 by Güell, who wanted a mighty mansion where Spain's queen regent María Cristina could lodge during her visit to Barcelona's 1888 Universal Exposition. She must have enjoyed herself, as Güell was ennobled as a count in 1908. No expense was spared on the Palau Güell: this was the period of Barcelona's stock market fever, when money spilled from the pockets of the wealthy like confetti at a permanent wedding.

In summer 1885 a cholera epidemic killed several hundred people in Barcelona. Güell and his large entourage were travelling around Europe, and Gaudí, with niece and father, spent the summer at Manuel Vicens's country house at Alella, in the hills near the city. In September, when the epidemic had abated and they returned, Gaudí and Güell set to designing the house. It is said they drew 22 designs for the facade, though only three survive. Work started in early 1886 and it was completed in a rapid two years, in time for the queen regent's visit.

The three buildings dealt with earlier in this chapter are original enough, but the Palau Güell beats them all. It made Gaudí well known. Press articles were written on the daring young architect. His name was cited in New York papers. Anecdotes started to circulate. One that comes in several versions was that a steward of Güell's complained that Gaudí was spending far too much – that the project was way over budget. Güell replied with magnificent munificence: 'Please tell Mr Gaudí he is not spending enough.' Güell wanted everyone to know that money was no limitation. Walls were marble. Ebony, tortoiseshell and ivory were set into wood. Exotic woods were inlaid with gold leaf. Another anecdote tells how a decorator proudly told Gaudí that he had saved money by using a piece of imitation marble that no one would notice. Gaudí, knowing he had no budgetary limit, rather priggishly told off the decorator for cheating: 'Art is a very serious business.'

Güell's six-storey house would not be the biggest in the city, but it would be unique. The Palau Güell still exudes the neo-Gothic influence of Viollet-le-Duc. Arab influences are evident, too. Yet the other elements of Gaudí's later style are already in place, only seven years after his qualification as an architect: the plasticity of the ironwork, wood and stone. For the first time in Gaudí, there are art nouveau touches, such as the curving furniture and bathtubs for which Gaudí's team was also responsible.

The greatest feature is the central salon that, like the nave of a cathedral, rises 20 metres (65 ft) through three floors, right up to the upper storey, where its dome bursts through the roof. Here Gaudí used catenary arches, which freed him from what he considered a fault in Gothic: the ugly flying buttresses that withstood the weight or 'thrusts' of the vaults. Rudely, he called these buttresses 'crutches'. The catenary arch allowed him to walk free. The huge room, encircled by a gallery and lit from above by beams of light through narrow holes that make the ceiling look like a starry sky, is the equal of anything Gaudí did later. Its sensuous luxury should lead to an Orientalist den, as in the Casa Vicens, but instead of this the architect built a private chapel and an organ. These were destroyed in the Civil War (1936–9).

The organ was placed on a floor above the great salon, so that music would spill like the starry beams of light over Güell's guests, who were entertained with concerts, poetry readings and exhibitions. This was a formal, princely art salon, not at all bohemian or avant-garde. Indeed, the Güell family hardly lived here, but used their house at the Finca Güell or, when in town, a nearby house at the bottom of Les Rambles. The *palau* was for soirées or guests. It was for show. There is a Gaudian conjuring trick implicit in the impression created on the visitor: the huge doors, the high salon and the tall columns make the building seem much bigger than it actually is.

Nevertheless, the mansion was habitable for guests, such as the queen regent and her retinue, if not altogether comfortable as a home. There were seven bedrooms arranged around the salon and several bathrooms. Güell and Isabel López's adolescent daughter, Isabel Güell, also encountered a problem. Musically minded, she was given a grand piano by her father on completion of the house. She complained to Gaudí that she couldn't find anywhere to put it, to which he gave one of his oft-repeated (and probably apocryphal) *bons mots*: 'Dear Isabel, take up the violin.'

In the other buildings in this chapter, Gaudí was decorating his roofs. In the Palau Güell, for the first time he built a roof where people could walk and look. From now on, his roofs became like another floor of his houses instead of just a covering of the building. God saw all parts of a building, but especially the roof, which he could look down upon. This roof is a cornucopia of eighteen multi-shaped and multicoloured ventilation shafts and chimneys (restored in 1994), 'an enchanted garden on the mansion's flat roof'.[26] If the roof was a surreal heaven, the cellar with its low vaulted ceilings, bare brick and dramatic darkness, with a curving ramp down which Güell's horses could be led gently to be stabled, was hell. Its destiny was hellish in reality, too, for in 1937, during the Civil War, the cellar was used as a *xeca*, a Stalinist prison for torturing revolutionaries. In 1945 the Güell family sold the mansion to the Barcelona Diputació (Provincial Council), and it became a theatre museum, a function more in tune with the building's drama.

Gaudí's team of stonemasons, bricklayers, tile-designers and -firers, jewellers, marble-cutters, carpenters, woodworkers, metalworkers and glaziers was extended for this huge, no-expense-spared project. The house was designed in its entirety – glass, furniture, doors, tiles, colours of the walls – with Gaudí like the player-manager of a football team, not just telling people what to do, but showing them. It was the attempt, in Cristina and Eduardo Mendoza's phrase, 'to fuse all the arts and conceive the building in its totality, characteristic of *modernista* architecture'.[27] It was also a triumph in its use of the latest industrial materials (gas lighting, cast iron, mass-produced brick and so on) not just for function, but to create beauty. Here, Gaudí was showing again that he was no addict of craft methods. He was following Viollet-le-Duc's insistence on using the most modern techniques to evoke ancient history.

Not everything is successful. Robert Hughes points to its 'kitsch – a Catalan parody of Scots Baronial, which clashes hideously with the Hispano-Moresque elements elsewhere'.[28] The style, says Colm Tóibín, is 'exquisitely incoherent'.[29] The paintings are poor. And it is not a place one would want to live. It is a symbolic building, showing off its owner's wealth. Perhaps the Trump Tower of its day, though with somewhat more original taste.

5

Religious Crisis

Just how much Gaudí earned for the three houses described in Chapter Four is unknown, but it is reasonable to assume that he was well-off by the time he finished the Palau Güell in 1888. He was in his mid-thirties, a successful professional man living in his country's capital. Ten years after qualification, he was well known in the city. He walked and rode, went to the theatre and the opera (he shared the Wagner-mania of *fin de siècle* Barcelona) and attended Eusebi Güell's salons. He lived with his father, niece and a maid in a first-floor flat at *carrer* Consell de Cent 370 in the Eixample – far from the slum rooms of the Old City of his student days in the 1870s.

During the period of his dedication to the Palau Güell, he was also working on the Col·legi de les Teresianes in Barcelona and the plans for the Bishop's Palace in Astorga. In addition, building was picking up pace on the Sagrada Família. In 1885, the first Mass was celebrated in the basilica's crypt. Gaudí's main office was transferred to the basilica in 1887, where he built a house on the corner of *carrers* Sardenya and Provença to serve as the home of the rector of the Sagrada Família, with his own workshop on the upper floor. The basilica's apse was completed by 1893, by which time Gaudí was also working on the ornamentation of the Nativity facade, dominated by his beloved vegetables and animals – the facade that would impose the basilica's presence on all Barcelona.

The spires that he was planning are reflected in the surviving drawing for a Franciscan mission-house in Tangier that was never built, which shows at least seven Sagrada Família-like towers. Gaudí travelled with Claudio López, the fabulously wealthy son and heir of Antonio López, to southern Spain in 1891, and it is probable but not certain that Gaudí crossed the Strait of Gibraltar to see the site in Tangier: if so, his first and only visit to Africa. López wanted to finance the building of the mission-house but in the end did not go ahead with the project, probably because of the Rif independence movement. Gaudí spent some months, if not years, working on and off on these plans.

He and his collaborators were taking on a number of minor commissions, alongside the famous buildings. For the 1888 Universal Exposition he did little, unlike other famous architects, especially Domènech i Montaner, but he did complete a prestigious commission to design an armchair for the queen regent when she opened the exposition. He also built a model of a pavilion of the Compañía Transatlántica Española, shown originally in a maritime exhibition in Cádiz, and exhibited it in the architecture section of the expo. While fully engaged in the race to finish the Palau Güell, he yet had time in 1888 to draw plans for decorating the Saló de Cent (Council Chamber) and the staircase of Barcelona City Hall, although the project was never implemented. Like all architects, Gaudí spent time on numerous projects that then came to nothing.

D'Ossó and the Teresianes

Successful and worldly though Gaudí was in the mid-1880s, by the end of the decade his religious devotion was deepening, as his employment for his next major project, the Col·legi de les Teresianes (Teresian School), suggests. Enric d'Ossó, founder of the convent school in 1876, found Gaudí sufficiently religious to remove the existing architect and to hire him to complete the building, when the ground and first floors had already been constructed. D'Ossó was a well-known crusading priest, inveighing against laicism, revolutionary politics, the loose morals caused by an Industrial Revolution that was weakening traditional values and a First Republic openly hostile to the Church. D'Ossó's missions were aimed at indoctrinating young children in the faith. On the fall of the republic in 1874, he had published a popular book that ran through numerous editions, *A Quarter-Hour's Prayer*. Gaudí was growing close to d'Ossó's ideas. Like so many of Gaudí's associates, d'Ossó was from southern Catalonia and, though not born there, was brought up in Reus.

Here the client was a religious order without a bottomless purse. The economic restrictions obliged Gaudí to produce a more sober building than the Palau Güell. The school-residence is a four-storey rectangular building on a horizontal plane. Austerity led to a building in bare brick and crushed stone, though Gaudí was not averse to *mudéjar*-like adornment by placing bricks at different angles and by slightly recessing the elongated windows, which repeat the shape of the pinnacles, almost battlements, on the roof. For this symmetrical, austere religious building, Gaudí returned to Gothic. Mackay wrote: 'The majestic simplicity of form and structure is evocative of the great pragmatic civil tradition in Catalan architecture, found in its late medieval stock exchanges, civic halls and religious buildings.'[1]

The inside is quite another question, as it was in the Palau Güell. Two inner courtyards ensure that light floods every room. The building's crowning glory is the space on the first floor, one of Gaudí's most renowned set pieces. Light pours in through a series of white parabolic arches to shimmer on the floor. Designed as corridors where the nuns could walk and contemplate, they were 'uncluttered and modern . . . a miracle of restraint'.[2]

This was also Gaudí's first building of a religious nature apart from the Sagrada Família, and, to d'Ossó's satisfaction, he really went to town with religious symbolism. The art historian Jaume Crosas counted the religious allusions in the building: 6 shields of Mount Carmel; Jesus named 127 times in tiles and 35 in wrought iron; and the initials of St Teresa, 87 times in tiles and 15 in wrought iron.[3] The wrought-iron entrance gate has the hearts of St Teresa and the Virgin Mary pierced by the spear of divine love.

Unlike Eusebi Güell, the stubborn, energetic and narrow-minded d'Ossó spent a great deal of time on site harassing Gaudí about costs. The architect finally forbade him entry, saying: 'Father, each to his own. I shall build houses and you go and preach sermons.'

It was a clash of two stubborn egotists. The increasingly religious Gaudí was kicking out a future saint, for d'Ossó was canonized in 1993 for his work in founding Teresian missions on three continents. Though Gaudí constructed a much cheaper building than his previous ones, d'Ossó, dedicated to austerity and poverty, was not wrong in his criticisms. Gaudí could not resist rather beautiful, but non-essential, brick spirals.

By the late 1880s Gaudí's days as a leading member of the Rambling Association were over, as his work occupied all his time. He persisted in horse-riding, but less and less. Nonetheless he remained a dedicated walker, trying to achieve an ideal 10 kilometres (6 mi.) a day. Joan Bergós reports him as saying: 'The feet hold up the head . . . Walking is essential to balance intellectual work and to lead to strong, restorative sleep.'[4] What spare time he had was spent on religion. In November and December 1889, for example, during work on the Teresianes School, he went on a retreat to a monastery in Tortosa.

His father was not just his accountant, keeping a record of his work and sending out bills, but shared with his son his methods of health care. Both became influenced by the water cures of a well-known German priest, Sebastian Kneipp, whose book *Meine Wasserkur* (My Water Cure) was translated to Spanish in the 1880s. Gaudí's father found that hydrotherapy improved circulation in his legs, curing his varicose veins. Gaudí, ever the extremist, took to scrubbing his body with cold water, even in midwinter. Unfortunately, or fortunately, Barcelona enjoyed a Mediterranean climate, so he could not follow Kneipp's lead in walking barefoot in the snow. He took to sleeping with his window open in any weather and claimed never to be woken, even by torrential rain, thunder or lightning.

Kneipp's views were not separate from his religious faith. He advocated simple food; water, not alcohol; and clothing made of natural fibres. Humans should try to live close to nature, which of course, for both Father Kneipp and Gaudí, was provided by God.

Grau and Astorga

At the same time as the Teresianes School, Gaudí was constructing another religious building. Once again, the Reus connection was key: the *reussenc* Joan Grau was Bishop of Astorga, in the province of León in north-central Spain. Grau had met Gaudí in Tarragona in the early 1880s, when his niece Rosita went to board with nuns there. At that time Grau commissioned from Gaudí an alabaster altar for his Tarragona church. Like d'Ossó he was part of the militant Catholic revival combating republicanism and anarchism. In December 1886, only two months after Grau had moved to Astorga to take over the bishopric, the episcopal palace burned down. Instead of using the diocesan architect, Grau turned to his old acquaintance from Reus. Throughout 1887, Gaudí worked on plans for a new palace. Grau liked them, but the Spanish government, which controlled the episcopal palace because it was a national monument, rejected the plans: 'the stairs were too narrow, the moat not wide enough, the columns too thin, the vaults too shallow.'[5] The government's expert was the Marqués de Cubas, who had designed Madrid's Almudena Cathedral. The irritated and irritable Gaudí showed his respect for Bishop Grau by redrawing the plans twice, both because of Cubas's objections and because, when in summer 1888 Gaudí finally visited Astorga, he found that the terrain was not as he had supposed from Grau's photos. It was not until June 1889 that the first stone was laid.

Whereas for the Sagrada Família he had succeeded in imposing his own design, in the case of the Astorga palace he found more obstacles. Despite Bishop Grau's unconditional support, Gaudí's argumentative, headstrong approach cut little ice with Cubas or the architectural experts of the Real Academia de Bellas Artes de San Fernando (San Fernando Royal Academy of Fine Arts), whose reports informed the Madrid government who held the purse-strings. Gaudí's characteristic improvisations caused numerous rows. In these years Gaudí travelled: some eleven trips to Astorga and nearby León, where he built a house known as the Casa Botines. Whereas Gaudí had had no interest in on-site work or seeing Díaz

Bishop's palace, Astorga, seen from moat below the Roman wall.

de Quijano when building the *Capricho* at Comillas, his relationship with Grau was quite distinct. In later years Gaudí emphasized the importance of Grau in his spiritual development. The bishop recommended books, and the two spent long hours discussing religion, not just architecture – or both at once, for the two were dedicated to working out how the new architecture could express the ideas of the religious revival. Religious buildings had to confirm and create Christians.

Here is one of several anecdotes told of how the bishop held Gaudí in such affection that he knew how to be diplomatic with the awkward genius. Gaudí suggested that the canopy over an altarpiece dating from 1562 be removed because it detracted from the altar's marble sculptures. Grau rejoined that the canopy was an essential part of Catholic liturgy. Gaudí insisted. 'Perhaps you are right,' replied the forbearing bishop. 'In this and in everything!' stated Gaudí. Grau agreed to refer the matter to higher authority, knowing that they would not agree to Gaudí's suggestion.

The palace is situated between Astorga's cathedral and Roman walls. Gaudí was keen for it to fit in with these imposing neighbours, but Jan Morris thought he had not managed too well, writing in *Spain* (1964): 'a bishop's palace built by Gaudí, like a cardboard ogre castle, stands grossly beside the pleasant cathedral of Astorga.'[6] For the neo-Gothic 'castle', Gaudí used white granite from nearby Bierzo, a stone so hard that it was difficult to twist or round its edges. Of all Gaudí's buildings, it is the least recognizable as his, though the idea that he triumphantly realized in the Palau Güell of a central space with the rooms of the building grouped around it is repeated here. The most unusual feature is the triple-arched entrance porch that supports a balcony and tower. This collapsed more than once during construction. Despite the mockery of architects round the state and the local crowds that gathered to watch the failed attempts, Gaudí's workmen – with him present to urge them on – finally succeeded in placing the keystone of the arches. Bergós quoted Gaudí's comments on this difficult structure:

Continuous forms are the best ones. Normally, supporting and supported elements are differentiated in a highly inaccurate way, but some are supported and supporting at the same time. Their differentiation creates imperfection.[7]

It is a comment that reveals how Gaudí conceived his buildings not as bits of Meccano to be screwed together, but as a flowing whole.

The Bishop's Palace at Astorga took four years to complete. Gaudí discovered the difficulties of working for the Spanish state, a notoriously slow payer. In a letter to Grau on 21 November 1892, he wrote:

> Until today, thank God . . . I have always been in the fortunate position of working for respectable clients who, in complete contrast to the State, understand that an artist has to live by his work and that it is hardly dignified to turn him into a beggar.[8]

He was expressing bottled-up rage at the obstructions to his work, rage that was fed too by his Catalan nationalism.

A year later, in September 1893, Bishop Grau died unexpectedly. He injured his leg and died of gangrene a few weeks later. Gaudí was present during his protector and close friend's last days. Grau's death was a life-changing shock for Gaudí. He resigned at once, leaving the palace without the white roof he had planned. It was poorly finished some years later. For the rest of his life Gaudí was bitter about his time in Astorga. The authorities asked him back, but he burned the plans and refused to go anywhere near the place. 'I would not even fly over Astorga in a hot-air balloon,' he is alleged to have said. His deep friendship with Grau, the hostility of the Madrid architecture mandarins and Astorga's conservatism all fuelled his Catalanist views.

While he was working on the Bishop's Palace, he supervised the construction of the Casa Botines in León, built between January and November 1892. León is only 50 kilometres (30 mi.) from Astorga, and Gaudí could travel between the two. The León house was commissioned by two Catalan textile magnates, business associates of Güell. Its name comes from the Castilianization of the name of one of the two, Joan Homs i Botinàs.

It was bold to build a neo-Gothic apartment block in León, whose cathedral is a jewel of Gothic architecture that would overshadow any competitor. As in Astorga, Gaudí's ideas clashed with local conservatism. He was criticized for using cast-iron pillars instead of thick, load-bearing walls. His behaviour did not help, as he brought his own workers from Catalonia and failed to explain his ideas to the local media. Despite contemporary newspaper articles stating that the building was unsafe, it has not fallen down. An innovation of Gaudí's, copying the Bishop's Palace at Astorga, was a moat or ditch around the building. This became common elsewhere in later years, as it gave more space and light to the bottom floors, making the building suitable for shops and businesses at and below street level. The free-standing, castle-like building was and is used for offices and flats. Its outer walls are thick and its windowsills

Casa Botines, in the centre of León.

sloping, measures to combat winter cold and snow. Indeed, Gaudí did not start building in winter, as it was too cold; all the stone and other materials were prepared, and spectators and the press were amazed at the speed of construction once spring arrived. Gaudí may have imposed a modern, neo-Gothic building on the centre of León, but was not at all ignorant of local conditions. Bergós recalled Gaudí saying:

> As it snows heavily here, I covered the house with a very steep slate roof and the turrets at an angle with pointed cones. I purposely left stones sticking out of the walls for snowflakes to stick to. At the first snowfall, curious passers-by were stopping continually to contemplate the attraction.[9]

It is a softer view of Gaudí. He was able to enjoy contemplating the passers-by contemplating his building. He also used local stone and placed a lion's head on the building (*león* means lion in Spanish), which showed goodwill to local sensibilities and, perhaps, some awareness of the poor impression his brusque character had given. Despite the severe facades of the building, close observation finds a host of what we have come to know as Gaudian details: sculpted iron fencing and adornment, turrets, curving *modernista* banisters, carved wooden ceilings and tall windows (which contrasted happily with the horizontal main lines of the building).

Finally, he designed and had placed over the main door a magnificent stone sculpture of St George slaying the dragon, sculpted by Matamala. St George (Sant Jordi) is Catalonia's patron saint, and this symbolism as a farewell Catalanist gesture to Astorga and León would not have been lost on the local burghers.

Breakdown

On his return to Barcelona in late 1893 after the death of Bishop Grau, Gaudí plunged into a deep pit of religious crisis. In truth, this had been boiling up for years. Professor Josep Pijoan, a contemporary of Gaudí's, wrote that the architect was 'criss-crossed with contradictions to an indescribable degree . . . His religious crisis lasted many years.'[10] While he was being sought for commissions, earning big money and becoming well known, he was becoming increasingly disgusted with the world. Gaudí had just turned forty, a time of staying as you are or of drastic change: of 'midlife crisis', as the term goes. As in anyone's life, there was no overriding factor to explain Gaudí's crisis, but a number can be posited.

Catalonia was in political turmoil. On 7 November 1893, the anarchist Santiago Salvador had killed twenty people by throwing an Orsini bomb from the 'gods' into the stalls of the Liceu, Barcelona's opera house. This was the most notorious act of anarchist terrorism, 'propaganda by deed', in these years and affected profoundly Catalan society, especially its conservatives.

A further and personal factor was Bishop Grau's death the previous autumn and Gaudí's exhausting conflicts in Astorga and León. Van Hensbergen suggests that the disgrace of Gaudí's poet-friend Jacint Verdaguer also destabilised him. In early 1894 Verdaguer was expelled from the Palau Moja, Claudio López's mansion on Les Rambles where the priest-poet had lived for nineteen years, because he had given away too much of López's money to the poor. Charity, dispensed by his priest from the back door of his mansion, was a source of pride to López, but Verdaguer was more radical, supporting with López's money some three hundred impoverished families. He was also veering into heresy, believing that illness was caused by diabolical possession. Along with other fanatical priests and a woman medium, he began to practise exorcisms.

It should also be remembered that the Sagrada Família, which was a thread throughout Gaudí's working life, was a temple to expiate the sins of the godless Barcelona populace. Like the leaders of the Catholic revival of his generation, such as d'Ossó and Josep Torras i Bages (the outstanding Catholic intellectual of Catalonia at the time, who in 1899 would become Bishop of Vic), Gaudí believed in the dualism of body and soul. This meant that to exalt the soul, he punished the body. Bergós reported that Gaudí told him: 'The mortification of the body is the joy of the spirit, as Dr

Torras i Bages says so correctly. And mortification of the body is continuous, persistent work. This is the most powerful aid against temptations.'[11]

Whatever the general background or particular catalysts, Gaudí began a long Lenten fast in February 1894. A fast was not uncommon among devout Catholics, but the headstrong Gaudí took it to extremes, as he did most things. A normal fast is controlled: it involves penitence. Gaudí's fast, tempting death, seems to show mental illness. This religious excess was self-destructive behaviour well beyond accepted Catholic norms.

Neither his father nor his close friend and doctor Pere Santaló could stop his hunger strike. Friends believed he was dying as he took to his bed, skeletal and lethargic. His physical decline was followed in the press. Workers from the Sagrada Família visited. One of them, Ricard Opisso, wrote that he was

> astounded by the squalor of the room. The wallpaper was peeling, because the architect had apparently forbidden anyone to touch it. His furniture consisted of nothing but a sagging bed and an uncomfortable cane sofa.[12]

The quote may well tell readers more about Opisso's anticlerical preconceptions than the literal truth. Gaudí was a rich man with a maid. 'Squalor' may be confused with simplicity.

Gaudí's fast was only halted when, after several weeks, friends called in Torras i Bages. Presumably, Torras i Bages argued that suicide was against God's wishes. The most famous of his many books, *La tradició catalana* (The Catalan Tradition, 1892), had recently been published. In it, he sewed together a conservative Catalan nationalism and Christianity, which gained ascendancy over a generation of Catalans, including Gaudí and other artists. His famous motto was *Catalunya serà cristiana o no serà* (Catalonia will be Christian or it will not exist), later carved on the front of Montserrat monastery, Christian Catalonia's spiritual home. Torras i Bages had sufficient spiritual and intellectual authority to oblige Gaudí to break his fast.

After 1894 the architect was often to be seen bearing a cross in religious processions. He attended Mass daily. Bishop Grau's recommendations became his bedside reading: liturgical books and Torras i Bages. With his customary extremism, he averred: 'The man without religion is a spiritually diminished man, a mutilated man.'[13] The fast did not diminish his spirit, but his body changed. The handsome, corpulent, upright man took on the bent, thin, white-haired shape of his old age.

6

The Spoiled Child of the Industrial Revolution

This chapter discusses the relationship of Gaudí with the particular fusion of styles and traditions that became known as Catalan *modernisme* or art nouveau.[1] It was part of a 'remarkable if brief and transitory' international movement flourishing in the ten years before and the ten years after 1900.[2] The style had several names: Modern Style in the United Kingdom, Stile Floreale or Stile Liberty in Italy, Jugendstil in Germany and Sezessionstil in Austria. It covered all the arts. In architecture, Gothic structures were lightened by Moorish minarets and detailed ornamentation modelled on nature's luxuriance, colours and curves. Like many new movements in the arts, it rejected the academy and wanted art to become more accessible to the people; though, unlike many such new movements, most of its main characters had little social conscience. Gaudí himself had no problem with the above ideas. In his early essay on ornamentation, he had written:

> Ornamentation has been, is and will be multi-coloured. Nature does not give us anything in just one colour. In vegetation, geology, topography or the animal kingdom, in none of these is there just one uniform colour.[3]

However, though today he is the most famous *modernista* architect, we should be aware that he rejected the term. He had no truck with the decadent symbolism of the 1890s often associated with *modernisme*. For example, the Catalan Impressionist Ramon Casas's famous painting *Madeleine* or *Au Moulin de la Galette* (1892), showing a woman worker after a hard day smoking a cigar and drinking a beer (or absinthe) in a bar, was anathema to the likes of Gaudí. In Catalan *modernisme*, a sharp line separated the Catholic artists and the bohemians. Apart from conservative prejudices against free women and bohemians' drunken antics, Gaudí had become a militant Catholic who supported the Church's vigorous counter-attack, led by Torras i Bages. These militants intervened in society through paternalist projects and promoted traditional life based on the idea of the *casa pairal*. The Catalan architect and historian Ignasi de Solà-Morales wrote:

> Gaudí and his circle of followers would have liked nothing less than being called *modernistes*, since this would associate them with ideas with which they would under no circumstances have wanted to be identified . . . the *modernista* heresy, condemned by ecclesiastical authority as dogmatic progressionism and impossible to reconcile with the official doctrine of the Catholic Church.[4]

There is an argument about art nouveau that is convincing, though it should not be taken too formulaically. Richard Burton, author of a travel book on Prague, summarized:

> Art Nouveau seems most to have thrived in marginalized political and cultural entities (Scotland, Catalonia, Belgium, and Bohemia/Moravia) and may be seen as a protest against provincialization by a dominant metropolis (London, Madrid, Paris and Vienna respectively) formulated in an international rather than a national style.[5]

Art nouveau was a common style at the end of the nineteenth and start of the twentieth centuries in several parts of Europe that were on the periphery of political power. This applied to Scotland, Latvia, Prague, Lviv (Ukraine), Cluj (Romania), the Balearic Islands and Valencia, as well as to Catalonia, the 'marginalized political and cultural entity' with the greatest amount of art nouveau architecture in Europe.

Capitalism developed in Catalonia before other parts of the Spanish state. Thus, by the end of the nineteenth century Catalonia's bourgeoisie was the wealthiest in a less developed Spain. Yet it was excluded from political power, exercised from Madrid in the interests of the Castile-based monarchy, military and landed aristocracy.

Art nouveau was the spoiled child of Catalonia's Industrial Revolution. The newly wealthy magnates, frustrated by their lack of political power, paid for art nouveau as the style of their houses. These businessmen and their highly cultured sons and daughters gave confidence to the Renaixença, the cultural and political renaissance that motivated the desire to show in stone and brick the rebirth of Catalonia as a nation. This class poured their money into buildings with an impact: the more ornate and showy, the better.

Gaudí was part of this generation that saw in art a way to build the Catalonia of the future, both recovering ancient glories and moulding the new. He (they) rejected the crass materialism of the Industrial Revolution and the revolutionary laicism of its workers, though of course not disdaining the money and new materials that this revolution provided.

Domènech and Puig

Though Gaudí is the most famous of Barcelona's architects, two of his contemporaries were equally celebrated at the time and are highlighted today in the tourist guides and art books: Lluís Domènech i Montaner (1849–1923) and Josep Puig i Cadafalch (1867–1956). Their prestige is reflected in the Illa de la Discòrdia (Block of Discord) on Barcelona's Passeig de Gràcia. Domènech was the main theorist of Catalan architecture in Gaudí's time, arguing for a new architecture consonant with the rebirth of Catalan nationalism. In his 1878 essay 'In Search of a National Architecture' ('En busca d'una arquitectura nacional'), after analysing several architectural styles, Domènech maintained that Catalonia's style had to be based on Islamic building elsewhere in Spain and on Gothic from the rest of Europe. Catalonia was the hinge where the two influences met. His first major building, in 1879, was a key precursor of *modernisme* and of Gaudí's work. In travel writer Michael Jacobs's words, this office of the publisher Montaner i Simon was

> the first building in Barcelona other than a market or railway
> station to take the form of an ironwork structure clad in brick.
> The element of fantasy, so necessary as well to Modernisme, was
> provided by the actual brickwork, which was inspired by the
> techniques of the Mudéjars.[6]

Domènech's writing and his work must have influenced Gaudí, but they were not friends. Though only three years older than Gaudí, Domènech was one of his teachers at the School of Architecture and is believed to have voted against Gaudí's graduation in 1878. This may be only a rumour, made credible by his later antipathy to Gaudí. Domènech was also held responsible for spreading stories about Gaudí's anticlerical activities in the late 1870s and early 1880s. Whether he was spreading the truth or exaggerating maliciously against a brilliant rival, even inventing the stories, is not clear. When Domènech became head of the School of Architecture in 1900, he expressed annoyance at how many students would visit the Sagrada Família to sit at the feet of Gaudí (quite literally) while the latter held forth on how 'Catalonia had been specifically chosen by God to take the long noble tradition of "arquitectura cristiana universal" on into the new century.'[7]

As well as an architect of renown, Domènech became a leading politician with the Lliga (League) de Catalunya, Catalonia's main conservative party from its foundation in 1887 until the Civil War. The Lliga sought both greater benefits for Catalan industry and sharper crackdowns by the state on Catalan anarchists. Gaudí sympathized with it but never joined. His dogmatic character and religious fundamentalism made him spectacularly unsuited to party politics.

It is worth citing Domènech's architectural achievements, quite the equal of Gaudí's in the arguments of many, including the organizers of 'Domènech year' in 2023, on the 100th anniversary

Lluís Domènech i
Montaner.

of his death. He built the great Palau de la Música Catalana, a
concert hall that is a riot of colour, statues and decoration cunningly
squeezed onto a relatively small site. Curiously, Domènech was
responsible for four houses in Reus, Gaudí's home town, whereas
the only recorded work of Gaudí there is the 1903 plan for a religious
sanctuary, which was never actually built. Gaudí became distant
from Reus after his family deaths, though throughout his life his
preferred friendships and business relationships were with *reussencs*
(Reus natives) and people from southern Catalonia.

Domènech's four buildings in Reus include the Pere Mata
psychiatric institute, an innovative hospital in large grounds,
designed so that fences and ditches to enclose the patients are
hardly visible. His other great social building was the Sant Pau
hospital in Barcelona, physically the largest *modernista* complex in

Pere Mata psychiatric institute, Reus, by Lluís Domènech i Montaner.

Catalonia (the site covers 13 hectares, or 32 acres). Its main gate is
now joined to the Sagrada Família by the pedestrian-only Avinguda
Gaudí, a rare diagonal cutting through the Eixample's rectangular
blocks. Sant Pau, like the Pere Mata hospital at Reus, was quite
the reverse of Gaudí's response to the poor. Sant Pau was the work
of an enlightened bourgeoisie, moving the medieval hospital out
from the Old City to a greenfield site on the slopes of a hill on the
edge of the Eixample. The Barcelona ruling class and authorities
paid for the hospital, while they abandoned the Sagrada Família to
its fate. They were keen to end the epidemics – not least of cholera
– that flayed the poor but also afflicted the rich. With his hospitals,
Domènech i Montaner showed a commitment to social welfare
not seen in Gaudí. Domènech fled, in the words of Hughes, from
the 'depressing, labyrinthine character that big general hospitals
share with prisons'.[8] Both Domènech and Gaudí loved light-filled
buildings, but the former rejected Gaudí's morbid obsession with
death and suffering and with the expiation of sins. Doubtless
he was a Catholic, like all right-wingers of the time, but he was
no fundamentalist. He may have been malicious toward Gaudí,

but Gaudí would try the patience of a saint (like d'Ossó) with his religious dogmatism.

The career of the younger Puig i Cadafalch spanned different epochs and styles. He ended up with the monumental neoclassicism of Barcelona's 1929 Exposició Internacional, but in his youth he was very much a *modernista*, as several famous buildings in Barcelona show. His is the Casa Amatller, beside Gaudí's Casa Batlló in the Illa de Discòrdia. Gaudí paid the younger architect the compliment of lowering one edge of the top floor of the Casa Batlló so as not to overshadow its neighbour. Gaudí was more courteous in the language of his buildings than of his mouth. Like his friend and maestro Domènech, Puig was a conservative politician, reaching the presidency of the Mancomunitat de Catalunya, a Catalan autonomous government with limited powers, from 1917 to 1924. He welcomed the coming to power of the Spanish dictator Miguel Primo de Rivera in 1923 because Primo de Rivera was going to outlaw the CNT (Confederación Nacional del Trabajo), the anarchist-led trade union. The dictator did indeed do this, but then in the following year he also closed down the Mancomunitat, deposing

Casaramona Factory, Barcelona, by Josep Puig i Cadafalch.

Puig. Unlike Puig, Gaudí was arrested in 1924 for demonstrating in favour of Catalan rights. Gaudí was no politician, but at least he did not lead Catalanism into a dead end as Puig did.

Puig i Cadafalch's very first house was the Casa Martí, built in the grounds of a vacated convent in 1896. This neo-Gothic *modernista* building became famous because on the ground floor the painter Ramon Casas paid for a café, Els Quatre Gats (The Four Cats),[9] based on Le Chat Noir in Paris. Els Quatre Gats, managed by Pere Romeu, was a meeting place for the artists of 1890s bohemia, a performance space and an exhibition area. It represented all the atheism, dancing, drinking, sexual licence and Parisian decadence that Gaudí abhorred. It was here that the young Pablo Picasso showed his early drawings in 1900. Casas, Catalonia's finest Impressionist painter and poster artist, drew all the known artists of the time, but significantly there is no drawing by him of Gaudí.

The Saint Luke Art Circle

The forerunners of the Quatre Gats crowd were the art festivals and events put on by the painter and playwright Santiago Rusiñol at and around his house in Sitges from 1892 to 1894, in which he and his friends brought international art to Catalonia. The young Puig i Cadafalch delivered a keynote speech there in 1894 in favour of modern art. Rusiñol put on the first performance in Spain of Maurice Maeterlinck's symbolist play *The Intruder* (1890). He bought in Paris and brought to Sitges two paintings by El Greco, at the time a somewhat devalued Old Master, and had them borne in procession through the town. These literary and painting modernists relished El Greco's heightened colouring, anguished faces and flowing clothes. This was the tone of the events, in Rusiñol's words: 'We would rather be symbolists and unbalanced, even mad and decadent, than debased and cowardly.'[10]

The playful iconoclasm of these wealthy young artists at Sitges did not appeal to Gaudí. While he was fasting near to death in that same 1894, a number of artists under the aegis of Torras i Bages were founding the Cercle Artístic de Sant Lluc, the Saint Luke Art Circle, based on the idea of the medieval guilds in which artists grouped together under the leadership of a priest. No more art for art's sake, no more female nudes, no more drunken poetry recitals. Catalonia would be Christian. Conventional images of 1890s art nouveau artists might lead us to think that the Saint Luke group were a small minority of conservative Catholics. Not so. They were serious people who wanted their art to influence an increasingly non-Christian world: the Saint Luke group statutes argue for the linking of art and faith, 'to re-establish the ancient Catholic guilds that so encourage the development of the arts and help strengthen mutual charity among the unfortunate'.[11] In addition, if you were looking for a church commission it was expedient to join.

A number of the members were well known, like the graphic designer Alexandre de Riquer (1856–1920), the Llimona brothers and Joan Maragall (1860–1911), Catalonia's leading poet after Verdaguer's death in 1902. As Josep (1864–1934) and Joan (1860–1926)

Llimona, sculptor and painter, and Maragall had attended Rusiñol's pagan, licentious festivals, they knew what they were talking about when they pleaded for a different kind of art. Gaudí sympathized with the Saint Luke group from the start and joined in 1899.

Nonetheless, the battle lines, though firm, were not total. Josep Llimona, despite his ardent Catholicism, exhibited female nudes in 1900 in Olot. The illustrator and painter Ricard Opisso (1880–1966) moved between the two groups. Aged twelve, he was apprenticed to Gaudí at the Sagrada Família and was immortalized as a trumpet-blowing angel on the Nativity facade. Later, Gaudí sponsored Opisso's entry into the Saint Luke circle to take drawing classes, but Opisso was also a friend of Picasso's and a habitué of the Quatre Gats.

Torras i Bages, already mentioned in the previous chapter in relation to Gaudí's Lenten fast, was the intellectual powerhouse behind the Saint Luke circle.

> Tall, corpulent, and as blind as a bat without his glasses, endowed with a deep resonant preacher's voice, Torras cut an imposing figure . . . the glare from his pebble lenses would make a liberal quake, a Protestant collapse.[12]

None of Torras's right-wing ideas is particularly original, but he was a writer and preacher of power. What Torras i Bages wrote was what Gaudí thought. Nor was Torras wrong: Catholic ideas and practice were in decline. Nietzsche thought God was dead; anarchism was winning over the workers' movement; the middle class was enjoying less religious observance and more sexual freedom; artists were painting nudes and . . . women smoked and drank in bars. Something had to be done! In some ways, Torras's ideas are the ultra-authoritarian Christian ideas of Carlism welded on to a Catalan national consciousness. Tradition was all-important; he eschewed novelty as diseased frivolity. Foreigners brought in contaminating ideas: against the craze for lewd flamenco from Andalusia, he posed the genteel Catalan *sardana* dance. Rural was good; urban was bad. The family and the language were the main supports of Catalan feeling. Love for the home and respect for the *casa pairal*, the rural, patriarchal family, guided by the village priest, should be the basis for social organization.[13]

Chapter Two mentioned Gaudí's only surviving document, what is known as the Reus Manuscript, in which he had argued along the same lines as Torras in favour of the *casa pairal*, but two decades before him. Both are reflecting a reactionary fantasy of an idealized rural life where the family in its house and land, guided by the father and the village priest, brings peace and stability. Of course, few can live like that: talk to the landless agricultural labourer, who needs collective organization and the destruction of the *casa pairal* in order to breathe. And even if the family does have the resources to live like that, the man's ideal life is based on the unpaid labour of women and children.

Though Gaudí and his fellow thinkers did not frequent Els Quatre Gats, they had the last laugh because, when Casas got fed up with financing the useless businessman and extravagant bohemian Romeu (he did not like to charge his friends for meals), the Quatre Gats went bust and the Saint Luke Art Circle took over the premises in 1903. The Saint Luke occupation of the Casa Martí lasted until the Civil War in 1936 and was influential in Barcelona's art world. Gaudí's association with it lasted all his life: there is a 1924 photo of him taking part in the Corpus Christi procession alongside several Saint Luke members, including the famous architect, inventor of *trencadís* and collaborator with Gaudí in the later part of his career, Josep Maria Jujol (1879–1949).

Gaudí also joined the Lliga Espiritual de la Mare de Déu de Montserrat (Spiritual League of the Virgin of Montserrat), a crusading organization founded in 1899. At the mountain monastery of Montserrat, Catalonia's main Christian shrine, the faithful queue to kiss the hand of the statue of the Black Virgin. Gaudí, in 1900, collaborated with Josep Llimona on the monumental Rosary of Montserrat, one of his few failed works. The two were commissioned by the Lliga Espiritual to link the ideas of Christ's Resurrection and Catalonia's Renaixença through images in a cave on the sacred mountain. It sounds blasphemous, but both

Gaudí, 1924. Corpus
Christi procession.

the League and Torras i Bages approved this fusion of religion and
Catalanism. Llimona's *Risen Christ* was to be lit by the rising sun's
rays on the spring equinox: a surprisingly pagan image, reminiscent
of Stonehenge.

The cave was blasted, but funding ran out after a few years.
Gaudí withdrew from the project in 1907 and it was not completed,
and not at all satisfactorily, until 1916. The lack of money for a
religious project brings to mind the Sagrada Família's funding
problems. The church's benefactors were fewer than it pretended.
Despite the seriousness with which Gaudí took his own religious
life and projects, he showed little interest in the cave. It ended up
as religious kitsch, with Llimona's statue hanging in the air, arms
outspread, above the mouth of the cave, more evocative of a music-
hall attraction than a religious icon, and with the flag of Catalonia
painted on the rock beside it.

The fashion, the rage for *modernisme*, embracing both the Quatre Gats and the Saint Luke sets, burned out in just a couple of decades. By the outbreak of the First World War in 1914, it was only some of the older architects who persisted in building in this style; 'Thereafter, what survived were the mere externals of a style that had become conventional mannerism, or a medium without a message.'[14]

The following fashion was neoclassicism, *noucentisme* in Catalonia. Some architects, such as Puig i Cadafalch, or the sculptor Josep Llimona shifted easily into this old style, though new fashion. *Noucentisme* was a reaction against what *L'architecture*, a leading Paris magazine, called art nouveau's 'drunkenness of forms . . . architecture of ice-cream cornet sellers'.[15] The *noucentisme* ideologues criticized *modernista* architecture as looking to the past, using old-fashioned stone and overloaded adornment. The new desire was for straight lines, concrete and glass, and minimalist adornment. Of course, reality was more complex than art historians' categories, with styles and fashions overlapping. For example, Jujol was working very much in the *modernista* style well into the 1920s: his Casa Planells in Barcelona dates from 1924, and his remarkable church in the village of Montferrí was started in 1926.

Gaudí himself was not usually a target of *noucentistes'* excesses of abuse against *modernisme*, whereas there were calls to knock down Domènech's Palau de la Música and 'clean the bourgeois houses of the Eixample of decadent ornamentation'.[16] Gaudí was not seen by the *noucentistes* as *modernista*. His riotous ornamentation was overlooked (quite a feat!). He was praised for his structural power and Catalan patriotism.

7

The Busy Years

The middle-aged Gaudí of the last years of the nineteenth century was a well-established architect, publicly known for his architectural and personal exaggerations. He was a leading light of conservative Catalanism. It might be thought after his spiritual crisis of 1894 that he would dedicate himself solely to religious contracts, but reality was more contradictory. Though profoundly religious and continuing to work on the Sagrada Família, his greatest civil contracts – and associated fierce fights about fees – were yet to come. The anticlerical artist Apel·les Mestres joked that Gaudí insisted he would accept only religious commissions, but then, when secular work was offered, he had to pray to the Virgin of Montserrat for guidance. 'The kind Virgin always capitulated and allowed Gaudí to take on secular work.'[1]

Though no longer a member of the Rambling Association, he still hiked in the hills with his elderly but fit father and walked everywhere in the city. He now went almost daily to evening Mass at the Sant Felip Neri church in an ancient, half-hidden square in the Gothic quarter, often walking the 3 kilometres (2 mi.) from the Sagrada Família. Gaudí was averse to having his photograph taken, but Joan Llimona persuaded him in 1902 to sit as the model for two paintings of Sant Felip Neri himself, still to be seen in the church.

Gaudí, his father and niece Rosita moved flat in these years, from *carrer* Consell de Cent 370, where he had suffered his religious crisis, to *carrer* Diputació 339, one street closer to the sea and a few blocks across the Eixample, still near the Sagrada Família. Rosa, like her absent father, drank too much. She treated her pains, arrhythmia and nervousness with the popular all-purpose herbal remedy *aigua del Carme* (Carmen water), concocted by nuns for women. The problem was that this apparently innocuous remedy, bought over the counter in pharmacies, was 55 per cent alcohol, slightly stronger than tequila.

Gaudí abhorred alcohol, and Rosa's problems did not make for a happy household. Gaudí, his father and presumably Rosa followed the dietary prescriptions of Father Kneipp, avoiding meat and eating small amounts of fruit, vegetables and grains. Olive oil or honey on bread, nuts and lightly boiled chard are reported as being Gaudí's habitual foods. He drank large amounts of water. In his pockets he usually carried bags of biscuits known as *panets de Sant Antoni*, small round biscuits stamped with a cross, which he nibbled frequently and distributed to whomever he was talking to. Formal meals used up too much valuable time, he thought.

A Flourishing Studio

Gaudí took on several major projects in these last years of the nineteenth century and first of the twentieth. It is not possible to deal with all his projects in strict chronology, for they overlap. The late 1890s saw him and Berenguer build the *cellers* (wine cellars) on Güell's estate at Garraf, on coastal cliffs south of Barcelona. In 1898 he started planning the chapel for the Güell village at Santa Coloma de Cervelló, though the first stone was not laid until ten years later. The same year saw him begin the Casa Calvet, in the Eixample but very near the Old City. In 1900 he started on the failed Monumental Rosary at Montserrat discussed in the previous chapter and the Bellesguard house in Barcelona. At the same time, he and Güell started to plan the garden city on the hill above Gràcia, the Park Güell.

Sometime in 1901, the Bishop of Mallorca, Pere Campins, visited the Sagrada Família. Enthused both by Gaudí's desire to draw the church closer to the people and by his architecture, the bishop invited Gaudí to reform Palma Cathedral. Between 1904 and 1913, Gaudí and his collaborators often took the boat to Palma. They did some necessary structural repair work on this jewel of Gothic architecture. However, Gaudí's ambitious project to simplify the choir by removing baroque additions (making it still-purer Gothic), and yet to complicate it with new stained glass, ceramics, windows, lamps and painting, ran into controversy. He was accused of betraying the original style. Despite Campins's support, the Church authorities halted the reform before completion. Nevertheless, Gaudí enjoyed his trips to Palma and friendship with Campins, which to some degree replaced his intimacy with Bishop Grau of Astorga.

Along with all these well-known projects, the architect's studio took on many other jobs. In 1900 he reformed the house at *carrer* Nou de la Rambla 32 (near the Palau Güell) of Pere Santaló, his friend and doctor; though Gaudí took little medical advice, convinced as he was of Kneipp's teachings and possessed of the masochistic belief that bodily ills and hunger were good for the soul. Santaló was a mild-mannered, quiet man whose two parents and all eight siblings died when he was eleven in the cholera epidemic of 1860. He had met Gaudí in the *tertúlia* (informal discussion group) of the *carrer* Pelai, and both became members and organizers of the Rambling Association. They remained lifelong close friends. They saw each other most days and often walked together. Apparently, Gaudí held forth on his religious and architectural ideas and Santaló complemented him by saying very little. To thrive, egotists need a quiet listener.

Gaudí also designed a new workshop for the Badia brothers, whose master ironworker Joan Oñós had done so much work for Gaudí. No money was exchanged: the Badia workshop paid Gaudí in kind. Lluís Badia expressed the pleasure of working with the exacting genius: 'None of us who've worked with Gaudí can escape his influence. Living next to that swelling sea of ideas, they soon become our own.'[2]

In 1899 Gaudí (or his studio) built a house at *carrer* Escorial 125, on the other side of Gràcia from the Casa Vicens, for the painter Aleix Clapés (from Reus; 1850–1920), who had worked with Gaudí on the decoration of the Palau Güell and would later supervise the interior decoration of the Casa Milà. This functional four-storey

Casa Clapés, Gràcia.

building in Gràcia is still there and must be the least noticed and most conventional Gaudí building in Barcelona.[3] He reformed a house in the Old City in 1901 for Güell's daughter Isabel and her husband the Marquess of Castelldosrius, but this was destroyed by Italian bombs in the Civil War.

Another building that has unfortunately disappeared, not due to fascist bombs but to business brutality, was the luxurious 'Vermouth Palace' on the corner of the Passeig de Gràcia and Gran Via, the Cafè Torino, built in 1902 for an Italian entrepreneur, Flaminio Mezzalama, who wished to introduce vermouth (Martini & Rossi from Turin, or Torino) into Spain. The Cafè Torino was notable for the collaboration of several architects, including Puig i Cadafalch and Gaudí, despite the latter's dislike of alcohol.[4] Gaudí designed an Orientalist room decorated with imitation tiles made from pressed cardboard – not so distant from the smoking-room and papier-mâché of the Casa Vicens nearly twenty years earlier. Despite its fame as a fashionable watering-hole and the success of vermouth, the Cafè Torino only lasted until 1911, when it was taken over and vandalized by a jeweller. The building is still there, but nothing remains of the *modernista* café. Gaudí also took on extremely small commissions at times. One such was the peacock window for a clothes shop in the Passatge de Ripalda in Valencia, Gaudí's only work in that city.

Alongside all this activity, Gaudí continued to work on the Sagrada Família. The last decade of the century saw the magnificent Nativity facade constructed and decorated. This baroque facade with three portals is carved in great detail, so needs time (and binoculars) to observe not just the Nativity story but its plants and animals. For the figures on the facade, Gaudí used local people, workers on the site and artisans such as Opisso. He made wire and wire mesh structures to then mould directly in plaster the faces of his victims. For the Roman legionnaire his people scoured the local bars to find a man nearly 2 metres (6 ft 6 in.) tall.

Gaudí's studio at the Sagrada Família included architects and sculptors, along with scaffolders, plasterers, bricklayers and labourers. These might be working on the Temple or be dispatched to the architect's other sites. One of these was the Cellers Güell,

Peacock window, Passatge de Ripalda, Valencia.

Sagrada Família, 1899.

boasting a wonderful position on the coast between Castelldefels
and Sitges, where the Garraf massif drops to the sea cliffs. There
is uncertainty over the exact date of these wine cellars and Gaudí's
part in them. For years they were attributed solely to Francesc
Berenguer, but Gaudí's close friendship with both Güell and
Berenguer, along with the quality of the work, suggest Gaudí's
participation. As to the date, earlier writers such as Zerbst and
Mackay place construction in the late 1880s, but Daniel Giralt-
Miracle states 1895–1901.[5]

Güell had bought the land in 1874, with three purposes: to
extract stone (used, for example, in the Palau Güell), to hunt and
to plant vines. The rough local stone used makes the wine cellars
seem at first glance to be an outcrop of the rocky promontory: the
fleeting impression of passengers passing on the Barcelona–Sitges
train. Close up, the outside is like a peasant's dry-stone wall. The
building is on five floors, two of which are underground for wine
storage. Parabolic arches on windows and doors, a characteristically

Cellers Güell, Garraf.

ornate cast-iron gate, a medieval turret and a plethora of vegetation all carry the Berenguer–Gaudí hallmark. Like Bellesguard or the Palau Güell, much of the building is severe, like a fortress with battlements, but then a richly decorated chapel and an open porch on delicate pillars with a rounded top overlooking the sea gives the building a contrasting and unlikely lightness. In skilful resolution of the clifftop's different levels, they brought the roof almost to the ground on one side. Zerbst wrote, 'This gives the work the shape of a tent, making it comparable with the pagodas of the far East.'[6]

Casa Calvet

While still working on the Cellers Güell, in 1898–99 Gaudí constructed the Casa Calvet at *carrer* Casp 48 in Barcelona. Assisting him as usual was Berenguer and Joan Rubió (born in Reus in 1870), who came to work with Gaudí at the Sagrada Família on his graduation from the School of Architecture in 1893, and on every project until 1905. After 1905 Rubió, tired of doing much of the work

Casa Calvet.

and seeing Gaudí receive all the acclaim (and some abuse), was appointed head architect for the Barcelona Provincial Council and became a considerable architect in his own right.

The Casa Calvet was Gaudí's first house in the Eixample. It is relatively sober-looking on the outside and won Gaudí's only municipal prize: for the year's best house, awarded by the City Council. That it was the only time Gaudí won this annual prize, despite the fame and glory of the later Casa Batlló and Casa Milà, suggests how much his style disconcerted the burghers of Barcelona. The clients were Juliana Pintó, widow of a textile manufacturer, and her three children. The main challenge of the block of flats was that it was not free-standing but had to fit between two other blocks. The basement was for storerooms; the ground floor for offices or shops (now, a fancy chocolate shop and a high-class Chinese restaurant); the noble floor, for the family; and the upper floors were flats to rent, flats that gave on to both the street and the back, as was the norm in the Eixample. Soberer than other Gaudí buildings it was, but it was hardly sober. Zerbst nuances: 'sober in general, but playful and symbolic in its details'.[7]

The flat front wall was decorated in a Catalan baroque style. The main front balcony and the graceful, undulating banisters are adorned with various kinds of wild mushrooms, to reflect the passion of Juliana's husband for mushroom collecting. It was common for *modernista* architects, building showy houses in the Eixample, to include references to the owners' tastes and source of money. Here, as well as the mushrooms, spinning bobbins top the columns by the street doors. The *tribuna* or main balcony was adorned with the characteristic cornucopia of fruit, a cypress tree and an olive tree, all sculpted in stone. As well as these trees, symbols of hospitality and peace, the building did not lack Catholic and Catalan symbols. As in the Casa Vicens, Gaudí had phrases written on the walls: *Faith, Love, Fatherland*, the motto of the *jocs florals*, and *Hail Mary most pure, conceived without sin*.

The structure is conventional, with stone from Montjuïc on the outside and brick within. The ceilings are Catalan vaults. Gaudí, in his passion for light and ventilation, had two inner courtyards constructed behind and in front of the stairwell and added two side courtyards for ventilation. This overcame the interior darkness of so many Eixample flats. The building had one of the first elevators in Spain. At the rear, he alternated closed galleries and undulating balconies, a trial run for his triumph ten years later in the Casa Milà.

Zerbst repeats the story that, when Isabel López visited the house with her husband Eusebi Güell,[8] she asked what the 'tangle' on the roof was. Gaudí replied that they were crosses, Christian symbols that were 'tangles and a problem for a lot of people'.[9] Whereas with his friends the wealthiest people in Spain he could be ironic, with the municipal architect, who complained that the building exceeded the permitted height, he showed picaresque disdain. Gaudí got out the plans, crossed off the cross and false wall at the top and sent Rubió round to the City Hall. The municipal architect was duly persuaded, but the roof was never lowered.

Interior decoration had been a key feature of the houses of Gaudí, the 'total architect', but now he added moveable pieces: the furniture. He designed the mirrors, benches and chairs for the owners' floor. Gaudí was beginning to experiment with curving chairs in the art nouveau style. Fitted together with cabinetmaker's skill without screws or nails, these are elegant, attractive and surprisingly comfortable chairs if you are the right size for them, for their curves fit the natural curves of the body more comfortably than the usual straight-backed chair. It is not possible to see inside the Casa Calvet unless you pay for a meal in the Chinese restaurant on the ground floor, but some of the house's furniture is now in other Gaudí houses or in the Gaudí House Museum in the Park Güell.

Bellesguard: Homage to Catalonia's Medieval Glory

The next year, 1900, Gaudí started work on the Torre Bellesguard, a house as different from the Casa Calvet as can be imagined. Gaudí switched styles from calm baroque to a most purely Gothic exterior. It is worth quoting what Gaudí told Bergós:

> I did the Doric columns of the Park Güell just as the Greeks would have done in a Mediterranean colony; the Bellesguard House is as profoundly Gothic as it is up to date; and the house of tenants on the carrer Casp [the Casa Calvet] is closely related to Catalan baroque. It's a question of immersing yourself in the time, the atmosphere, the resources and capturing their spirit.[10]

Bellesguard means 'beautiful view', something that can be appreciated from the flat roof, which overlooks the plain of Barcelona. The site contained two ruined towers and a wall that date from when Count Martí (Martin) 'the Humane' of Aragon had his summer palace there. Martin is of special significance in Catalan history as he died heirless in 1410, making him the last of the line of Catalan-Aragonese monarchs. Two years later the Council of Casp chose a king from the Spanish-speaking Trastámara dynasty. Many nationalists date the start of the decline of Catalonia from that moment when the language of power became Castilian Spanish. Gaudí, deeply immersed in the historical significance of Bellesguard, built the house as a medieval castle. On its own site, surrounded by a large garden – though much smaller now than it was in Gaudí's day – Bellesguard is extremely impressive: tall, slim, dark, with a tower topped by the four-pronged cross characteristic of several Gaudí buildings. The cross represents the cardinal points and also the fruit of the cypress, a tree with the religious connotation that its height and straightness help souls ascend to heaven. Below the cross are painted the stripes of the Catalan flag: here he fused Catalanism and Christianity rather better than in the Monumental Rosary at Montserrat that he was engaged in, on and off, at the same time. Under the Franco dictatorship, ferociously hostile to Catalan nationalism, the flag was painted out. It was repainted after the dictatorship, which explains why it now has a brighter colour than the cross. As at the Casa Calvet, the words *Hail Mary, conceived without sin* were placed above the rounded archway (imitating ancient fortified Catalan farmhouses) and wrought-iron gate that serves as the main door.

Neo-Gothic had always been the principal element of Gaudí's eclectic style. At Bellesguard, assisted again by Rubió, he did not mix Gothic with curved lines. The lines are straight; the outside is a severe fortress in a vertical plane, its windows pointing upwards, rising to battlements with a walkway for sentries, then to the tower. The interior, in contrast, is adorned by mosaic to create gentler, colourful, curving, light-filled surroundings, though, unlike most

Torre Bellesguard. Music room on the top floor.

Gaudí houses, there is not a lot of decoration. And there is no original furniture. This is because the house became an orphanage run by the PSUC (Catalan Communist Party) in the Civil War, a cancer clinic afterwards and a private house until 2018, when the Guilera family sold it for €30 million to an insurance company. Like the Casa Vicens, it has only recently been opened to the public.

Here Gaudí, the total architect, extended his control of all facets of the house to include the garden. Bellesguard's garden was something of a trial run for the Park Güell, which he was planning

Gate to the Finca Miralles. Statue of Gaudí.

at the same time. At Bellesguard he used inclined stone columns to hold the weight of the earth on a slope, later so striking a feature of the Park Güell.

The client for Bellesguard was another widow, Maria Sagués. As often, work was slow because Gaudí was engaged in numerous other projects and because he was always improvising on the job. Costs ballooned. Gaudí declared completion in 1909, five hundred years after Count Martin's wedding there in September 1409. The marriage was a failed attempt to find an heir, as the Count's four legitimate sons and first wife had predeceased him. As with many of Gaudí's projects, the building was not completely finished. Domènec Sugranyes completed it in 1916. Sagués's heirs then sold it, some say to avoid bankruptcy – the kind of rumour or reality often associated with Gaudí's enormous bills.

At the same time as he was building the Casa Calvet, Gaudí designed, and the Badia brothers' workshop constructed, the wall and gate of the Finca Miralles (though now there is no estate behind the gate). Hermenegild Miralles was a bookbinder and decorator who had worked with Gaudí on the Casa Vicens and later on the Cafè Torino. He ran a company that supplied pressed wood and pressboard (a kind of compressed cardboard) tiles to the construction industry. Standing on fat, distorting stone legs, the gate's roof twists as if in agony: 'a capricious shell', in Zerbst's phrase.[11] Since 2000 a life-size statue of Gaudí has stood by the gate, at Passeig de Manuel Girona 55, not far from the Finca Güell dragon gate.

Park Güell: An Island Apart

The Park Güell, a huge tourist attraction today, slopes up the eastern sea-facing side of a hill behind Gràcia. The land was bare scrub when Güell bought it. Gaudí's trees and shrubs have made it the most beautiful, luxuriant park in Barcelona. 'Park' is written in English, for its inspiration came from the garden cities popular at the time in England, such as Hampstead Garden Suburb, which Güell had visited. Though usually called a 'garden city', the park was really a gated community. The idea was that the rich, threatened by anarchist-led social agitation, would buy the sixty triangular plots, where they could each build a house with a garden and a view. Güell and Gaudí saw the city below as a place of sin and class hatred. The park was conceived as a refuge on a green hill, looking down on the dangerous, revolutionary city.

Light, gas, a market, a chapel and leisure areas would all be supplied. Inner walls between houses would be low, but the whole complex was surrounded by a high wall, and (such was Güell's influence) a police station was constructed near the front gate. The enclosing wall, the first feature of the park to be built, ran up, down and along the hill. It was constructed with irregular large stones and covered with ceramic tiles hanging towards the outside. This perimeter wall of solid and hard stone to keep out the populace contrasts with the light and joyful tiling that runs throughout the park. As with the Palau Güell and Bellesguard, austere and severe exteriors conceal softer, luxurious interiors.

Eusebi Güell's desire for a piece of paradise on a hill away from the class struggle had its roots in his own history. Born in 1846, he was old enough to remember the killing in the 1855 general strike of Josep Sol i Padrís, his father's friend and the managing director of his textile factory, El Vapor Vell. More than thirty years later, just before Christmas 1889, the factory's technical manager, Ferran Alsina, was fired on from the dark when he was walking home. Alsina escaped unhurt, but the incident along with the memory of the death of Sol i Padrís stimulated Güell to move the factory away from Sants to Santa Coloma de Cervelló and, a few years later, to plan the Park Güell. In times of increasingly dangerous labour conflicts, Güell was looking for both a safer place for his factory and a safer place to live.

The Park Güell was a spectacular failure. Only three plots were sold, and Güell abandoned the project in 1914. His heirs sold it to the City Council in 1922. Today, though, it is so popular that tickets have to be bought online and entry is staggered to prevent the whole park being overrun. The park is Gaudí's happiest creation. A pair of whimsical lodges that look like life-size gingerbread houses from

Park Güell. Lodge.

'Hansel and Gretel' flank the entrance. These are the caretaker's lodge and administration building, built to attract potential investors. Hughes thought it probably frightened them off. You understand at once, after climbing the hill past the police station now occupied by anti-tourism anarchist squatters ('Tourist, you are the Terrorist' is painted on the wall), why the park was so popular among post-1960s hippies.

Park Güell. Tunnel of Stone.

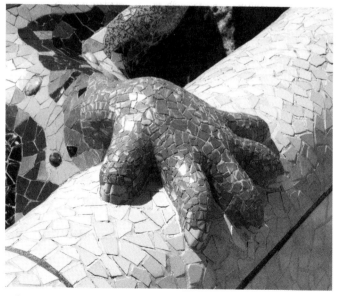

Park Güell. The gecko's foot. *Trencadis*.

Park Güell. The house by Berenguer where Gaudí lived.

Gaudí created triangular flat areas at various levels for the projected houses. For the terracing of these different levels he used inclined columns to hold back the earth, as he had at Bellesguard. They form long, shaded tunnels. These columns' unsmoothed stones look like tree trunks. Visitors know they are stone, not wood, but are nonetheless drawn to caress them to check. The tops of walls bulge as if they were the round tops of Mediterranean pines. Gaudí admired and copied the dry-stone walls built by the peasants of his childhood in the Baix Camp without mortar and from the materials to hand. Gaudí's aim was to imitate nature and become part of it, not to dominate nature as an orthodox French-style garden does. This would be blasphemy, for God disposed Nature.

The centre of the park is an enormous plaza raised on 86 Doric columns. The mosque-like open part beneath was to be a marketplace for the community. The tops of the columns look squashed by the weight above. Stone water-drops ooze from the edges of the ceiling. Around the plaza twists a long bench-parapet adorned with *trencadís*, the mosaics of broken tile stuck into mortar to form abstract patterns of riotous colour, with a magnificent view over the city below. Pevsner wrote:

> The snakily undulating back of a long seat running along the sides of a large open space was faced with bits of broken tile and crockery in arbitrary patterns as effective as any invented by Picasso.[12]

Trencadís also dominates on the great staircase below the plaza, forming the huge gecko or dragon from whose mouth the water of the cascade spouts. Gaudí had a giant water cistern built underground, but above the dragon, which collected water from the hill and plaza above. The water from the rain was filtered through sand and pebbles before running down pipes in the columns to the cistern. So purified was this water that Güell set up a mineral water company in 1913.

Josep Maria Jujol worked with Gaudí on the *trencadís*. Jujol, like Berenguer and Rubió, was another of the talented architects who worked with Gaudí and went on to design original houses themselves. Gaudí told all his workers to bring any broken pots they found to the site. Passers-by and journalists were amused and amazed to see the distinguished architects sifting happily through heaps of broken glass, tiles and shattered pots. These collage-mosaics can be seen now as forerunners of later styles such as cut-up technique in Dada in the 1920s and the colours of abstract art. Many years later, Gaudí's fellow Catalan Salvador Dalí liked to sit on the multicoloured bench round the plaza. Gaudí's rendering in stone of soft objects such as vegetables, fruit and fishing nets foreshadows the oozing, liquid rocks of Dalí's paintings. Another rather unusual influence was on the Argentinian writer Julio Cortázar (1914–1984), who always referred to the ideas that came to him for his fragmented novels and stories as 'pieces of mosaic'. When he was three years old, his mother often strolled with him through the Park Güell and his imagination was inflamed by these many multi-form colours.[13]

The park, a commercial failure, became a vision of paradise, where humans imitated nature to make nature part of their lives.

No plants or trees were imported: all the vegetation is indigenous. Gaudí refused to flatten parts of the hill to create paths. Instead, the paths ran over viaducts or through gorges. Earth excavated was used in the walls. Gaudí prided himself on using materials found on site.

By 1904 the two lodges had been built, and in 1906 Gaudí bought one of the houses, the show house to attract clients that is today the Gaudí House Museum. This first and only property that Gaudí owned was constructed not by him but by Berenguer. The explicit reason for the move was that his father now found climbing the stairs to their Eixample flat difficult. It was also a step for Gaudí away from the city, from society. His family – Rosa, his father and Vicenta, a young woman servant – moved to the house. Gaudí was to live there longer than anywhere else in his life: until 1925, when he moved permanently to the Sagrada Família. Each morning he attended Mass in the church of Sant Joan in Gràcia before walking on to the Sagrada Família. In the evening he often strolled in the park with Santaló or with Güell, who moved to the old manor house in the park a year after Gaudí. The new household lasted only a short time, as his father, Francesc, died on 29 October 1906, at the age of 93. Francesc had been a walking companion, friend and accountant for his son. His death left Gaudí alone in the new house with Rosa and Vicenta.

The Chapel in the Woods

After the attack on Ferran Alsina in 1889, Güell moved rapidly. He used some land his father had bought by the Llobregat river many years before to build a new factory some 20 kilometres (12 mi.) south of Barcelona. The huge boiler was moved from Sants, the factory there was closed in 1893 and all the workers were sacked.[14] He hired new workers from the countryside, whose background and experience made them less politicized (he hoped) than the city proletariat.

Textile factories could be found all along the Llobregat. In the 1890s there were as many as 75 on the Llobregat and on the Ter river to the north. The rivers flowed fast off the Pyrenees and drove the factory turbines. Catalonia suffered from a lack of coal, and what coal it had was of poor quality. Water-driven factories saved their owners from the economic burden of having to import coal. Many of the owners of these mills built industrial villages (*colònies* in Catalan) to house their workers, making them dependent on the boss for their homes as well as their jobs. Though these *colònies* were expensive to build, the initial investment was justified as they guaranteed for decades a relatively docile workforce, isolated from the militant trade unionism of the cities. Conditions in some *colònies* were probably little better than on the Cuban slave plantations where several textile magnates had actually made their money. But many, like the village that Güell eventually built beside his factory at Santa Coloma de Cervelló, were paternalist projects to educate the workers in Catholic values. Profits could be conserved and the boss's life protected, at the same time as he could feel he was dousing class conflict by religious education and benevolent provision.

Güell's industrial village came into being much more slowly than the factory. Actual planning did not start until 1898. While Berenguer and Gaudí were still working on his wine cellars at Garraf, Güell began to discuss the project with them. Between 1898 and 1911, a hundred workers' brick houses, with sanitary facilities and small gardens, were built. Each house measured at least 55 square metres (600 sq. ft), a standard living space for most middle-class European families today and a huge improvement on the slum rooms and flats of the time. Berenguer was responsible for the school and the doctor's house, while Rubió built Ca l'Espinal, the factory manager's house. Though it was Rubió and Berenguer who were responsible for building the village, their and Gaudí's styles were so interlinked that one imagines that all three contributed to all the houses. The village had not only a school but a nursery, choral society, football team, shops, a café and an Athenaeum (a cultural centre where literacy was taught or classes on science and art were held). One could say that this was the 'garden city' that the Park Güell failed to be. Santa Coloma de Cervelló was a far-reaching social experiment, influenced by the industrial villages in the United States or elsewhere in Europe, such as Sir Titus Salt's at Saltaire in West Yorkshire in the 1850s. The village recalled Gaudí's adolescent plans for Poblet monastery and the Mataró cooperative, though Santa Coloma was Catholic and paternalist, not anarchist and cooperative.

No paternalist Catholic village seeking to create a new race of non-class-conscious workers would be complete without its church. The village already had a small church, but Güell wanted something bigger. Gaudí designed and oversaw the building of the crypt, the only part of the church to be completed. The crypt is not in the village but on an adjacent low hill in a pine wood. It does not dominate the village, unlike the tall churches in the middle of most of the rivers' *colònies*. Yet it dominates subtly by being hidden in the trees. Despite its being unfinished, many experts view it as Gaudí's finest work.

There is a sketch by Gaudí of the church that might have been built on top of the crypt but which never was. It has several towers

The doctor's house, Colònia Güell, by Francesc Berenguer (with input from Antoni Gaudí).

like upside-down ice-cream cones with crosses on top, reminiscent of the Sagrada Família, though these towers are rounded at the top, similar to Catalonia's holy mountain of Montserrat and the drawing for the unbuilt 1892 mission in Tangier. The sketches for the crypt are close, too, to the surviving sketches and project for the also unbuilt Hotel Attraction (1909) on Manhattan island. This extraordinary hotel project was unknown until 1956, when Joan Matamala published an article. It would have been a treat to see Gaudian towers among (or towering above) New York's skyscrapers.[15]

Though the crypt was planned as early as 1898 along with the rest of the village, work on it did not start until 1908. Unlike some of Gaudí's clients, Güell was extremely patient, both because his political and religious opinions were close to Gaudí's and because he recognized Gaudí's genius.

In a hut in the woods by the village, Gaudí and his collaborators spent long hours and years experimenting with the catenary arches he had used at the Palau Güell and, most exquisitely, at the Teresianes. This was at the same time as he was working out how to build the Sagrada Família towers. He relied on the mathematical expertise of Joan Rubió until 1905, when Rubió left him. The collaborators were trying to distribute the weight of the roof without pillars and without outer buttresses. Gaudí told Bergós:

> Without the full-scale test of the rounded shapes, helicoid in the pillars and parabolic in the walls and vaults, that I achieved at the Colònia Güell, I would not have dared use them in the Sagrada Família.[16]

They built a 4.5-metre-high (15 ft) model of the crypt at a scale of 1 to 10. The model was then turned upside down and hung by string from plasterboard nailed to the ceiling of the hut. These cords hung down naturally in gravity. Then different weights were attached to the cords, altering the symmetry of their fall. Other cords were attached to the original ones as cross-strings and to the ceiling board, forming an extremely complex design. Small canvas or cotton bags were hung from the strings to shift the parabola of the arch. As Hughes wrote: 'All the loads in them were pure tension – the only way string, which has zero resistance to bending, knows how to hang.'[17]

Participants, such as Llorenç Matamala, recalled spending hours adding and subtracting shotgun pellets to and from the bags in order to adjust the weight. 'With two rulers and a cord one generates all architecture,' Gaudí proclaimed.[18] His throwaway comment is unlikely to have been appreciated by his colleagues and employees slaving away in the studio-hut in the woods. On one occasion rats chewed through the string, and the company of highly skilled technicians and visionary builders (often the same person) had to start again.

When the mechanical skeleton, each part dependent on the others, was complete, Gaudí had it photographed and then followed the photos, turned upside down, to build the structure. It was an empirical method. He conceived it 'in terms of the angles and planes generated by a web of compressive and tensile forces'.[19] They were like tensed muscles. Though the photos in the museum at Santa Coloma look quaint, it was revolutionary architecture. Until computer modelling in recent decades, no one had done this. Even today no one else has done it, because Gaudí followers such as Santiago Calatrava use reinforced concrete. Gaudí used only brick and stone. Why? Because he was building a structure as close to nature as possible. Each column was different, as trees are in nature, not polished to uniform smoothness. Gaudí was using primitive materials to surpass Gothic.

The 42 columns of the crypt lean very sharply but have no counterweight. The chapel's great beauty derives, in part, from this seeming defiance of gravity. In addition, unlike most Catholic churches, the chapel contains no images or sculpture to distract from the structure itself. The decoration is reserved for the 22 windows of stained glass and cast iron, some in the colours and shape of butterflies. Thus, Gaudí reduces the separation between outside and inside: the pine wood seems to enter the church. The constantly fluttering, multicoloured beams of light that pour

Colònia Güell. The crypt in the woods.

through the stained glass into the chapel provide the decoration. The local rough, yellowish stone of the sober exterior again merges the chapel into its surrounds.

The interior of the chapel is wholly visible from the door. All the seats are positioned with a view of the altar, with minimal

Colònia Güell. Entrance porch to the crypt.

interference from the basalt columns. It is like theatre in the round, an impression enhanced by the passageway round the back of the altar and two aisles through the seats. All attention is focused on the altar. Alastair Boyd highlighted that Gaudí was following a medieval tradition:

The wide vault and the columnless space seem to have satisfied a desire rooted in the Catalan character for a great open uncluttered space in which the congregation and the priest could communicate without unnecessary barriers.[20]

It makes one think, too, of the huge nave, the biggest in Europe, of Girona Cathedral, creating a wide space without pillars, and of the light-flooded cathedral of Valencia. These are, structurally and psychologically, a long way from the dark, brooding, oppressive cathedrals of Castile.

An open porch stands outside the entrance, again half inside, half outside. A bench runs round the inside of the porch. This traditional feature of Mediterranean churches was a place where, during Mass, animals (donkeys or dogs) could wait or men could sit and chat. If you ever attend a Mass at Christmas or Easter in Spain, you are likely to be surprised by how women pack the pews inside while men stand and smoke by the open door and in the porch. Their hum of conversation competes with the priest's sing-song. The porch reminds visitors, too, that Gaudí was not just a religious fanatic but a practical militant. He wanted to draw the Church, and God, closer to daily life.

Work stopped on the crypt in 1915 due to economic problems caused by the First World War. That was that, then: a crypt and a porch, but no church. Today it is seen as a masterpiece, but the reaction of early viewers to so strange a building was confused. Nikolaus Pevsner ignored Gaudí in the first volume of his *Pioneers of Modern Design* (1936), but in the 1970 edition grappled with the crypt in surprise and puzzlement:

It is in the Colónia Güell and its amazing, fascinating, horrible, and inimitable church . . . that walls are first set in motion, windows appear in the seemingly most arbitrary positions and the seemingly most arbitrary forms, that columns bend or stand out of plumb, and that the craftsman is encouraged to leave work rough.[21]

8

Everything Flows

The four great achievements of Gaudí's mature period are the Park Güell and the crypt of the Colònia Güell, two works linked to flight from the city's class struggle, and two houses at the very heart of the bourgeois city, the Casa Batlló and Casa Milà, on opposite sides of Barcelona's most fashionable avenue, the Passeig de Gràcia, 'the cosmopolitan boulevard created by the *modernista* bourgeoisie'.[1] These four works – a park, a chapel and two houses – are UNESCO World Heritage Sites.

This first decade of the twentieth century saw Gaudí in his splendour, fusing the chaos of his eclecticism into a new whole. Let us quote again his excellent biographer Gijs van Hensbergen:

> This is Gaudí's great paradox. For the further he travelled away from the idealism of his youth, and the stricter a Catholic he became and the more antiliberal, pessimistic and obsessed with suffering – the more glorious his architecture grew.[2]

Harmony and Discord

Josep Batlló was yet another textile manufacturer. He had owned one of the first houses on the Passeig de Gràcia, built in 1877. The architect was Emili Sala i Cortés (1841–1921), one of Gaudí's teachers at the School of Architecture. By the turn of the century Batlló was looking for a more spectacular house, especially as the chocolate manufacturer Antoni Amatller had hired the young Puig i Cadafalch to build the house next door in 1898. The Casa Amatller was so spectacular that it made Batlló's house look tawdry. One should not underestimate the competitiveness between Barcelona's wealthy industrialists. They united to combat the anarchist-led working class, but fought with each other to build the finest house on the street. The City Council's planning committee did not allow Batlló to demolish and rebuild his house, but it did grant permission to reform it. Batlló was introduced to Gaudí by Pere Milà, impresario of the Barcelona bull-ring: almost all Gaudí's jobs were gained through personal contacts. Gaudí took up the challenge and started work in November 1904.

Out of respect to Puig i Cadafalch, Gaudí lowered his original plan for seven floors so as not to overshadow the Casa Amatller, but there was no getting round the clash of styles. This is the Illa de la Discòrdia, the Block of Discord, on which the houses by Gaudí, Puig, Domènech and Enric Sagnier argue with each other. Gaudí 'wins' hands down, not least because the bad-tempered genius created a happy, smiling house designed by someone in absolute command of his style – his mature, unified style, beyond Gothic or Baroque. The other houses are outstanding:

> Domènech, rational with eclectic decoration; Gaudí caught up with a total idea that flows through and gives a Baroque shape to the whole; Puig, patriotic and European, adroitly steering between the medieval and the classic . . . Posterity is fortunate to have a joint monument to them, and to modernista architecture . . . majestically dominating the Passeig de Gràcia, harmonious in their 'dissonance'.[3]

The original Casa Batlló was gutted except for the floor levels: Gaudí did not respect the City Council's edict to only 'reform' the building. Every wall was rebuilt with the utmost care and avoidance of any abhorred straight line. As always with Gaudí, light filled the building. Whereas in the Casa Calvet, Gaudí had built extra internal courtyards, here he devised three tricks to bring light even to the lowest floor. The two inner courtyards were coated by some 15,000 blue tiles, some in relief to throw the light downwards and the ones

Block of Discord. Casa Amatller (Puig i Cadafalch) and Casa Batlló (Gaudí).

at the bottom paler and paler. Second, the courtyard's windows became bigger, the lower they were; and, third, the courtyard itself opened out, the higher it got (as in the Teresianes). The inner courtyard's wide windows served for both light and fresh air: they had wooden ventilation panels beneath.

As in the Casa Calvet and Casa Botines, the ground floor and basement were for commercial purposes; the proprietors had the main floor; and the remaining flats, with a separate entrance, were to let. The luxuriously decorated main floor is a wonder. The dining room has a womb-like fireplace surrounded by walls of mini-ceramics. Its great living room gives on to the street; its folding oak door is decorated with stained glass. Though this was a civil commission and Gaudí did not have to follow religious strictness, inevitably the roof was adorned with Catholic and Catalanist symbols: a tower on a garlic bulb, with a cross bearing the symbols of Jesus, Mary and Joseph; and the theme of Catalonia's Sant Jordi slaying the dragon. The chimneys on the flat roof are adorned by Gaudí–Jujol coloured glass and ceramics.

The front wall was where Gaudí and Jujol really showed off and their imaginations took flight. The pillars, like bones of fine sandstone, move seamlessly into what seems like soft, billowing skin on the upper sections. Gaudí achieved a building where different parts are not eclectically put together but where each part flows into the next. The wrought-iron balconies are shaped like skulls or masks and cling to the wall 'like nests on rocks'.[4] Light is a prime concern not only within the building but on the facade. Rounded, multicoloured ceramics hang from the wall like fish scales. The

The shimmering front of the Casa Batlló.

architecture historian Maria Antonietta Crippa wrote, 'Window frames curve like flowering branches and ceramic tiling shimmers like reptilian skin.'[5]

Robert Hughes, meanwhile, wrote that 'the Casa Batlló's facade is an architectural equivalent to the shifting, luminous crusts of airy and watery color in Monet's water-lily paintings.'[6] The smooth wall appears to undulate, like the skin of a snake in water; its colour changes in shifting light, with cloud or blue sky, between morning and evening. In part, this was achieved by increasing the number of stones and pieces of glass towards the higher parts of the building, and in part by placing pieces of glass so that they gradually lose intensity, until they fade into the light grey background. Imagine Gaudí on the street, where now the tourists stand peering up, shouting to his workmen on the scaffolding just where to place each fragment of glass or tile. We are still a few years before the rise of Surrealism in the 1920s, but this is surrealist architecture.

So complex a building needed many skilled workers. The common view of Gaudí as both a haughty individualist who didn't suffer fools gladly and a solitary genius has a lot of truth in it, but he was also capable of leading a team of collaborators and inspiring close friendship in a number of people throughout his life. Collaboration was essential on a project like the Casa Batlló. The architects Berenguer, Rubió and Jujol are well known; the Badia brothers, heirs to the business of the master ironworker Joan Oñós, too; but there were many others. Sebastià Ribó worked on the ceramics; the main engineer was Josep Bayó i Font, admired for his mathematical calculations; woodwork was in the hands of cabinetmakers Casas & Bardés. All of these firms had their own workers, putting up scaffolding, hanging doors, sticking on tiles and slates, roofing, bricklaying, carting stone. Gaudí was no solitary artist like Picasso in his studio or Woolf in her study. He was the boss of a large business with several permanent workers and dozens more hired for each project.

The cartoons and gossip columns of the time comment that Gaudí did not get on with Batlló's wife, Amàlia Godó, and that husband and wife argued often about the unusual decor and

Casa Batlló. The noble floor.

furnishing of their flat on the noble floor.[7] One believable story was that Gaudí asked Amàlia how many men and how many women would be living there, for he wished to make ergonomic chairs shaped differently for men or women. Amàlia refused to have chairs according to gender. She got her way. If you visit the Casa Batlló today, you will see that the main flat is full of Gaudí-designed furniture, but photographs of the time show that the internal furnishings were mostly in a nineteenth-century style: straight-backed chairs, not Gaudí's curving ones. Gaudí's taste and design were undoubtedly ahead of his time, but Amàlia was the client, and she wasn't paying to live in a museum of the future.

Casa Milà

The handsome, ultra-rightist dandy Pere Milà, the person who introduced Batlló to Gaudí, had married an older and richer woman, Roser Segimon, the widow of an *indià*. When Gaudí had finished Batlló's house, Milà and Segimon (also from Reus) hired him at once. She had inherited from her first husband a house on a corner plot a bit higher up the Passeig de Gràcia, and they were going to build a house even bigger and better than Batlló's. The Batlló house was a reform, but for the Casa Milà, Gaudí demolished the existing house to start from scratch. By the time Gaudí had completed his masterpiece, Milà and Roser Segimon must have wished they had never heard of the man.

The Casa Milà is geological, a rock, unlike the Casa Batlló's subtle, ethereal facade of shifting light. The Catalan painter (and amateur boxer) Joan Miró said that he always strived for a painting that would strike the first-time viewer like a punch on the nose. The first sight in real time of the Casa Milà, however many times seen in images beforehand, knocks most people out. Colm Tóibín wrote: '[Gaudí] followed the shape of waves and the shape of molten rock of the mountain of Montserrat. He used cut stone, with hammered surfaces which appear to be the result of natural erosion.'[8] David Mackay wrote of 'the wave-like rhythms of the irregular walls draped with sea-weedy balconies',[9] while the house leaflet talks of 'a huge wave set in stone'. Hughes thought of the Casa Milà as 'a sea cliff with caves in it for people. Its forged-iron balconies, with their wreathing and flopping tracery, are based on kelp and coral incrustation.'[10] 'A hulk marooned from another era', said Van Hensbergen.[11] The novelist Joan Perucho wrote of 'a kind of stone lung, breathing gently'.[12] 'Delirious and edible', sighed the delirious Dalí.[13] 'It could be compared with a sheer wall in which African tribes had excavated caves,' wrote Rainer Zerbst.[14] No one is quite sure what it is, but everyone knows it is something special.

This huge apartment block with the facade that punches the first-time visitor on the nose was built on the corner of the Passeig de Gràcia and *carrer* Provença. The blocks of the Eixample are square, but not totally square, for each corner (*xamfrà*) is bevelled or chamfered. Thus, the Casa Milà has three sides: the main, but narrowest, facade facing the Passeig de Gràcia at an angle, and two flanking parts facing the two streets mentioned. South-facing, it receives the sun all day long. The facade stretches along the two streets and the *xamfrà* for 85 metres (280 ft). The plot, measuring 1,835 square metres (20,000 sq. ft), is four times bigger than the

Casa Milà. 'Huge wave set in stone'.

Casa Batlló. Milà and Segimon's flat on the main, noble floor is the biggest I have ever heard of: 1,323 square metres (14,000 sq. ft). The four remaining floors had three or four flats to let, each between 300 and 500 square metres (3,200–5,400 sq. ft). The block's great size and peculiar shape allowed Gaudí to create two large internal patios, letting light pour into the flats. In the middle of the *xamfrà* is the huge main door, with a ramp leading down to the first underground garage for cars in the city. The Palau Güell had a ramp leading underground for horses, but Gaudí grasped quickly that the rich would not be travelling any more in horse-drawn carriages, except to their funerals.

The porous, pitted front walls of stone look like a beach moulded by waves. The house has always been called popularly La Pedrera (The Quarry) because of its size and the honey-coloured limestone from the quarry at Montjuïc. Unlike at the Casa Batlló, here there are no multicoloured ceramics, sculptures in stone or shimmering light, only the undulating wall and the enormously complex wrought-iron balconies, designed by Jujol and forged by the Badia brothers. It is a simpler house than the Casa Batlló, but what attracted Gaudí was the size of the site. Here he could break free from the limitations imposed by the rectangular, standard-size Eixample plot that he had experienced with the Casa Calvet and the Casa Batlló.

Gaudí's bare rock is offset, contrasted and completed by Jujol's ornate balconies. Chapter Seven mentioned Jujol's skill on the Park Güell *trencadís*. Jujol started working with Gaudí in 1904 while still a student at the School of Architecture. Born in 1879 in Tarragona, he was yet another collaborator from Gaudí's area of southern Catalonia and, just like Gaudí, worked his way through architecture school. Though he started as an employee, he rapidly became Gaudí's collaborator. Barcelona's leading art historian today Daniel Giralt-Miracle affirms rather strongly that:

> Jujol had an absolutely artistic and surrealist nature, with a sharper degree of madness than Gaudí. The first person to discover Jujol's talent was Gaudí who sucked the blood out of him and absorbed his talent. He made him his. Often we don't know where Gaudí starts and where Jujol ends.[15]

Jujol was not 'absorbed' by Gaudí, though. Rather, Jujol influenced Gaudí in a more surrealist direction. Gaudí was a famous architect 27 years older than Jujol but had absolute faith in him and allowed him more freedom than he gave to anyone else in his workshop except Berenguer. He recognized in Jujol an equal. The balconies of the Casa Milà are not repeated images, such as Joan Oñós's famous palm-leaf fence at the Casa Vicens, but are variations on a theme. Hughes raved about them:

> It is quite certain that no previous forged-iron balconies ever looked like the ones that embellish the outer walls of the Casa Milà, with their ungeometric curlicues, their forms derived from kelp and sea-snails, their general air of delicious homage to all the wonders that once lived beneath the surface of a great port.[16]

Jujol and Gaudí caused the Badia brothers further headaches, as the metalwork design could change from day to day. The two architects could spend all day happily discussing and arguing about the metalwork or *trencadís*. Jujol brings to mind his contemporary, the sculptor Julio González, who attempted to make solid iron float, to free sculpture from mass and weight. Both were imbued with Catalonia's long tradition of ironwork. González was, like Jujol, an abstract sculptor whose works are based, however distantly, on real objects: the human figure, in the former's case, and nature in Jujol's. Among the beaten metal, coils and twisted bands of iron, Jujol and Gaudí placed birds and flowers (not everything is from under water, as Hughes alleged).

Gaudí used the latest methods in the structure of the block of flats, giving the lie to the *noucentista* attacks that he wanted only to work in outdated brick and medieval stone. An iron skeleton was erected and the front wall was hinged onto it, which meant he had no need for load-bearing walls. It gave him freedom to create the famous undulations. The distribution of flats was also original: no flat or room was rectangular. Gaudí used the unusual shape of the site to fit together flats and rooms like the misshapen pieces of a jigsaw. He was also able to drop the level of the balconies below that of the flats, so that the inhabitants' view of the street was not impeded by Jujol's fancy ironwork. The facade and balconies were to be strewn with hanging plants: Gaudí planned an irrigation system that was never installed.

Casa Milà. Undulating roof.

The roof is another floor for God to look down on, as in so many of Gaudí's houses. Here the chimneys and ventilators are adorned with white mosaic and coloured ceramic, colour that makes up for the lack of colour on the facades. Several chimneys huddle together like hooded sentinels. They are not straight, but twist powerfully. Others are capped playfully by broken green bottles. The roof's floor is not flat and the low walls flow like waves, which makes walking across it feel slightly perilous, like walking on the deck of a boat at sea or through a dream landscape. From here you can look along the *carrer* Provença to the towers of the Sagrada Família. The Casa Milà was Gaudí's last civil contract. On its completion in 1912 he would devote his energies to the Expiatory Temple.

The interior decoration was as sophisticated as in the Casa Batlló: catenary arches supporting the roof, pillars rough like tree

Casa Milà. Curving ceiling, top floor.

trunks, and delicious details such as door handles shaped to be opened by the left hand, as the right would hold the key. Painted, swirling walls and ceilings look like the fleshy insides of a body. As you come down from the bright, usually sun-baked roof into the dark attic, now the exhibition floor, you are struck by arches that curve out from a knot across the ceiling like palm fronds or a fan opening. Everything of course is curved, leading to the poet Josep Carner's adaptation of the joke of Gaudí recommending that Isabel Güell take up the violin because her piano would not fit in the Palau Güell. The variation tells of a tenant complaining to Gaudí that the curvy walls made it impossible to find a good place for her dog kennel. 'Madam,' replied the architect, by now beyond caring, 'purchase a snake.'

There are many more stories about the Casa Milà than earlier projects. This is because Gaudí was famous after the Casa Batlló, and Catalan society lined up either in approval or to tell tall stories about him. Cartoons and satires appeared in the press. Postcards of his houses were mass-produced. In the 1907 general election, the newly formed Catalan nationalist coalition Solidaritat Catalana, led by Enric Prat de la Riba, had won 41 of 44 seats, a never-to-be-repeated triumph of Catalan nationalism. The cause was near-universal disgust at the trashing of the offices of a satirical magazine, *¡Cu-cut!*, by the Spanish military in 1905. Gaudí's prestige was such that he had been invited to stand in this election. Puig i Cadafalch was sent to approach Gaudí again after his initial refusal. Gaudí refused again. He supported Solidaritat but was not interested in party politics. He saw his contribution to building the future of Catalonia in a literal way: building buildings.

Another legendary story of the house that throws light on Gaudí's character and working methods is about a fellow architect who, on visiting the site, commented critically to Gaudí that he just couldn't believe the amount of improvisation taking place on the job. Gaudí fished in a pocket of his ancient, ill-fitting suit and drew out a crumpled piece of paper. He smoothed it out and replied: 'Improvisation? Here are my plans.' Sometimes the severity and intransigence of this bad-tempered fanatic makes one overlook his dry humour. It is present in his buildings, such as when painted or sculpted animals peer from unlikely corners, and it is there in such anecdotes as this.

Flanking the main entrance are two columns with thick, 'elephant-foot' bases. City inspectors found that these and others protruded onto the public pavement. With his customary disdain for public officials, who were quite correct in demanding that he comply with city ordinances and not steal public space for private use, he said that he would cut off the offending part of the 'elephant foot' as if it were a piece of cheese, but place a notice beside it: 'Mutilated by order of the Barcelona City Council'. Work was suspended for a time, but, as had occurred previously, Gaudí's wealthy clients forced the council to back down.

The building of the Casa Milà was beset by legal problems from the start. The council objected to the invasion of the pavement not just by 'elephant feet' but by the hoardings enclosing the building site. Though work was officially suspended, building went ahead without permission. In fact, the application to start building work was only approved when the fourth floor was already complete. Van Hensbergen found the documents in the City Council archive and calculated that the Casa Milà was only legal for four weeks of the 36 months' construction![17]

As Gaudí's greatest house moved towards completion, much around him was deteriorating. Segimon and Milà were increasingly irritated by the escalating budget. Gaudí's father had died at the start of the construction. The press mocked the hubris of his extraordinary building. One should not exaggerate his troubles, for he enjoyed the all-day sessions on site and the problem-solving with Jujol and with Josep Bayó, the engineer responsible for the very complex calculations needed. And he had constant friends, such as Pere Santaló, with whom he walked most days. He had a new friend, too: Alfonso Trias, son of the only other people to have bought a house in the Park Güell, who often met him after work to walk home. After Pepeta Moreu, all his friends were male.

Churches in Flames

It was a political event that caused Gaudí most grief: the *Setmana tràgica*, or Tragic Week, as it is now generally known. In July 1909 an insurrection broke out in Barcelona against the conscription of troops to fight in Spain's colonial war in Morocco. Women protested on the quay as men were taken on board ships to go to Morocco. Some conscripts refused to go. Many threw into the sea the religious medals that upper-class women had pressed on them. On the night of 24 July, a general strike was called. On 25 July, the employers locked out their workers. On the 26th, a revolt erupted. Police stations were attacked. Civil government collapsed, as some soldiers refused to fire on demonstrators. For Gaudí and his fellow thinkers on the right of the political spectrum, the *Setmana tràgica* was a terrible disaster. The riots took an anticlerical turn, hardly surprising given the strong support of the Church for the status quo that held millions in poverty. By 1 August, when troops drafted in by the central government had suppressed the uprising with artillery and rifles, some eighty churches, monasteries and Catholic welfare institutions had been destroyed. Though between 100 and 150 demonstrators died, only two or three priests and eight police were killed.

The *Setmana tràgica* split the unity of the 1907 election and divided still more clearly anarchists and Catholics. No longer would it be so easy for middle-class youth to flirt with café-table anarchism, as the Quatre Gats bohemia had done. Eusebi Güell and Claudio López had mining interests in 'Spanish' Morocco, which meant that these great patrons of the arts were militantly in favour of more troops being drafted to defeat the Rif independence fighters. The two industrialists were explicitly targeted in the slogans of the *Setmana tràgica*. In the most powerful image of the week, corpses of the Hieronymite nuns were disinterred from the convent in the Plaça del Padró and borne across El Raval to be left outside the Palau Güell and López's Palau Moja on Les Rambles. The dead nuns' feet were found to be tied, a practice of the order. This was taken, though, as evidence that young women were confined and tortured in convents. Gaudí and his friends and fellow thinkers were profoundly shaken by this blasphemy and by the deep hatred that class-conscious workers felt for the Church.

Gaudí spent the week in various ways: he walked round the Park Güell with Santaló or visited Alfonso Trias. The park was indeed a refuge from which they could watch the smoke rise from the burning city. Sant Joan in Gràcia, where he attended Mass, was burned. He is also reported to have gone to the Sagrada Família, fearful it could be attacked. It was not (though it would be in July 1936). The only loss of Gaudí's work was the destruction of an altarpiece that he had designed for the Jesús i Maria school. With characteristic stubborn insouciance he insisted on walking through the crowds, hearing the whine of bullets and sidestepping barricades, to go to Mass at Sant Felip Neri.

The *Setmana tràgica* confirmed Gaudí in his commitment to a temple to expiate the sins of Barcelona's working class. For a religious person, the burning of churches was a deeply depressing catastrophe. The uprising caused him an antepenultimate falling-out with Milà and Roser Segimon. Gaudí insisted on his project of putting a giant cross on the roof that would glisten all down the Passeig de Gràcia in tribute to the Virgin of the Rosary, but Roser and Milà said no. Understandably, though in Gaudí's view weak-mindedly, they feared that such religious ostentation might attract attacks by anarchist-led mobs.

The penultimate falling-out was that Milà and Segimon refused to pay Gaudí the rise in cost from the initial budget. They had already paid heavy fines for Gaudí's breaches of city planning regulations. There were several factors in this overspending: Bayó found the blocks of limestone were so heavy he needed special machinery to raise them; Gaudí and his helpers, as was their habit, improvised on the march; and, as usual, work was slow because Gaudí, Jujol and Bayó were meticulous. Gaudí left the project in umbrage, just as he had left the Casa Batlló, and sued Milà for his final payment. In 1916, surprisingly, he won and Milà was ordered to pay Gaudí 105,000 pesetas plus costs. It is said that the house had to be mortgaged to pay the compensation. To add insult to injury, Gaudí then immediately seized the moral high ground by donating to a convent the money Milà was obliged to pay him.[18]

The ultimate falling-out was artistic and a severe case of cutting off one's nose to spite one's face. Segimon may have been from Reus, but on taking possession of her 1,300-square-metre flat, she emulated Amàlia Godó of the Casa Batlló by having all the Gaudí interior design stripped out and redecorating in a French classical style. Roser Segimon had a later sympathizer in (dare we say) the rather philistine Pevsner:

> Who would be ready to live in rooms of such curvy shapes, under roofs like the backs of dinosaurs, behind walls bending and bulging so precariously and on balconies whose ironwork might stab you at any moment?[19]

I wouldn't mind . . .

9

Stubborn as a Pig

In 1910 the extremely energetic Gaudí fell ill. The shock of the *Setmana tràgica*, the continuing decline of his niece Rosa and the Casa Milà saga all contributed to bringing him low. The mental crisis of 1894 manifested itself in a fast. The 1910–11 physical collapse, associated also with mental suffering, was brought on by an attack of brucellosis, probably caused by drinking unpasteurized milk. Among its symptoms was severe rheumatic pain, reminiscent of his ailments as a child. Dr Santaló persuaded him to take a rest cure and go on a diet to build up his strength: several friends thought he was suffering from malnutrition. Bishop Torras i Bages arranged for Gaudí to stay in the mansion of a wealthy parishioner in Vic, while nuns were engaged to look after Rosa. It was probably the most comfortable lodging that Gaudí had ever had, accustomed as he was to sleeping in a cot with the windows open and eating nuts and lettuce dipped in milk. His several lunches with Torras i Bages in the Bishop's Palace were probably a little richer. Not all was rest and food. While in Vic, Gaudí designed lamp posts for the city. Two were constructed to his design (with the characteristic cross on top) but removed in 1924.

There is an interesting witness to Gaudí's three weeks of May 1910 in Vic, the pharmacist Joaquim Vilaplana, who showed him round the city and left a record of their conversations. Vilaplana did not like Gaudí, who was 'a good Christian, but stubborn as a pig'. Arguing with him was disagreeable because he argued 'as if he were giving hammer blows'. Gaudí's opinions were narrow-minded.

True art was only found round the Mediterranean. He inveighed ridiculously and at length against Rembrandt, van Dyck ('third-rate decorators') and Michelangelo (the Sistine Chapel was 'insensitive').[1] Gaudí had always been convinced of his own qualities as an architect and dogmatic in his views. His illness and the various blows suffered since the death of his father exacerbated his difficult character.

In 1910, one event cheered Gaudí. Güell organized and paid for an exhibition of his work at the Grand Palais in Paris, the only one anywhere in Gaudí's lifetime. It ran from April to June. Furniture, plans, models and photos of his buildings were featured. It was 32 years since Güell had spotted Gaudí's display cabinet in that same city. The exhibition gives the lie to the idea that Gaudí was an isolated, misunderstood genius: he was recognized internationally in his lifetime. Gaudí was nervous about the exhibition, but critical response in France was positive. Gaudí liked to appear indifferent to criticism, but he was not averse to praise. International recognition was particularly welcome just when the fashion for both *modernisme* and his own style (*post-modernisme*, one might say) was giving way to *noucentisme*. Recognition in France was welcome, but Gaudí's illness meant he did not go to Paris.

He returned from Vic to his austere life, but in spring 1911 he had another serious attack. His mental equilibrium was not helped by the suicide in November 1910 of a friend, the novelist Raimon Casellas. This time, Santaló persuaded Gaudí to spend four months with him at a hotel in Puigcerdà, a Pyrenean town on the border with France. No visits were allowed. Gaudí felt so ill that he wrote his will on 9 June. His team continued work without him. During this period, Jujol worked on the colourful, lively serpentine bench at the Park Güell. Maybe its joyfulness reflects Jujol's delight in freedom from his all-controlling boss.

Dante in Stone

Towards the end of his convalescence at Puigcerdà in 1911, Gaudí travelled to Toulouse to visit Viollet-le-Duc's restoration of

Gaudí, 1910, at the time of the Paris exhibition.

Notre-Dame du Taur. His disappointment in his great early mentor was confirmed. 'Let's go back,' he told his companion Bergós. 'These buildings have nothing to teach us.' He had been at Viollet's Carcassonne in the 1870s, and this later visit confirmed to Gaudí what has become a common view: Viollet wrote great theory, but he was no great architect. Viollet knew it all but lacked the 'instinct' that the greatest artists have of knowing just where to place a piece. Bergós quotes Gaudí (remember, no one remembers exactly what someone said many years before, so the words are not literal):

> Gothic art is imperfect, half resolved. Its stability is based on its being constantly propped up by flying buttresses. It's a defective body supported by crutches. It does not have full unity. The sculpture is not fused with the decoration.

He went on, thinking back to Poblet perhaps: 'What proves that Gothic buildings have deficient plasticity is that they transmit the greatest emotion when they are mutilated, covered with ivy and lit by the moon.'[2]

Gaudí recovered from his illness, but another blow awaited him. His niece Rosa died in January 1912, aged 36, only a year older than her mother when she died in 1879. From this time on until his death, living alone apart from his maid Vicenta and, later, nuns who came to clean once a week, he was increasingly depressed, ill-tempered and rude. The deaths of his close friends Francesc Berenguer in 1914, Bishop Pere Campins in 1915, Bishop Torras i Bages in 1916 and Eusebi Güell in 1918 did not lift his mood. 'My good friends are dead; I have no family and no clients, no fortune nor anything. Now I can devote myself entirely to the Church,' he announced in melodramatic self-pity.[3]

Gaudí belonged to the Torras i Bages-led wing of the Catalan Church, which, in the spirit of Pope Leo XIII's 1891 encyclical *Rerum novarum*, believed that the Church had to approach the new working class to draw them away from revolutionary anarchism. There are reports of Gaudí, on more than one occasion, accosting priests in the street and telling them they should abandon their comfortable lives and get their hands dirty on social projects with the poor. This idea led to the construction in 1908–9 of a small school for the children of Sagrada Família workers and local working-class children. It had three classrooms and a chapel. Opened in late 1909, its purpose of instilling proper religious education in the poor was given renewed urgency by the *Setmana tràgica*. Damaged in the 1936 revolution, the school was restored, though not too well, in 1937. In 2002 it was moved to its present site outside the temple to make way for ongoing work. The school's structure of undulating brick walls and characteristic Catalan vaulted roof makes it a simple and solid building. Le Corbusier admired and sketched it on a visit in 1928.

With all his other work – the controversial reform of Palma Cathedral, the crypt at Santa Coloma, the Casa Milà and the Park Güell – stuttering to a standstill, Gaudí dedicated himself in body and soul to the Sagrada Família. He was confirmed in his commitment in 1915, when the papal nuncio Cardinal Ragonesi, on a visit to the Sagrada Família, told him before a large crowd: 'You are the Dante of architecture. Your magnificent work is a Christian poem carved in stone.'⁴ This was the highest praise, coming from the representative of God's representative on earth.

Despite Ragonesi's words, by 1914–15 hardly any money was coming in. Barcelona's ruling class loved to spend fortunes on their fancy houses, but they were not so eager to finance a temple. The dependence on donations made the basilica's economy 'overwhelmingly languid', in Josep Pla's ironic phrase.⁵ The fewer the resources, the higher the architect's imagination soared. He spent years making and remaking models and plans. The crypt at Santa Coloma provided him with material for study. How was he going to achieve the enormous building in his mind? As he abandoned Gothic, Gaudí was working out how to build the height he wanted without flying buttresses. The Sagrada Família, he had told Vilaplana, 'must stand without crutches, because I don't like crutches or walking frames'.⁶

Domènec Sugranyes, who was from Reus and had worked with Gaudí from 1896 (and was to succeed him as the Sagrada Família's architect), highlighted in a text of 1923 the greater 'repose and

Gaudí, 1915, sharing a joke with Cardinal Ragonesi.

The elderly genius.

calm that satisfies the spirit' in the structural simplicity of the Sagrada Família, as against the complex play of forces in Gothic.[7] The temple's columns turn like tree-trunks and push the facade upwards.

Gaudí became increasingly obsessed with both solving the architectural problems of the basilica and raising cash. This latter obsession drove away all but employees and faithful acolytes. People crossed the street to avoid him, as he tended to importune acquaintances and passers-by for money. An anecdote told by the architect Cèsar Martinell has Gaudí urging a well-wisher he has waylaid to make a sacrifice and give him money for the basilica. 'No, no, it's a pleasure. No sacrifice,' replied the polite donor. The relentless Gaudí insisted that the poor man increase his donation until it *was* a sacrifice. He thundered at his victim: 'Charity not based on sacrifice is not true charity and is often simple vanity.'[8]

The basilica had accompanied Gaudí for almost his entire working life. The crypt was first used for a Mass in 1885 and was completed in 1891. The walls, windows and spires of the apse were constructed between 1891 and 1893. By 1900 the Nativity facade was nearly finished, as were the north window of the transept, the cloister and the Rosary door.[9] In 1903, the upper part of the transept with spires at the top was completed. In December 1921, money was found to lay the first stone of the nave. On Gaudí's death, only the crypt, the apse, three spires and most of the Nativity facade were finished.

Nativity: Light and Joy

The Nativity facade faces northeast, lit by the rising sun. Gaudí had been advised to build the Passion facade first, as this faces the city centre and so would show off the temple's attractions better, but Gaudí believed that the Passion was too depressing an event to feature as the 'advertisement', the first facade to be built. While the Nativity facade is filled with flowers and birds, of light, of joy, with rounded shapes, the dark, harsh Passion facade was to show the cruel horror of the Crucifixion, and thus the great sacrifice of Jesus, in brusque, angular shapes. The third monumental facade, the Glory, the biggest of all, faces south.

Gaudí planned eighteen spires for the Sagrada Família: one each for the Twelve Apostles, the Four Evangelists, the Virgin Mary and, the highest tower, Jesus Christ. If and when it is completed it will be the highest church in Christendom, at 170 metres (560 ft). The nave is 95 metres (310 ft) long. The semi-circular crypt measures 30 × 40 metres (100 × 130 ft). Everything is huge. Gaudí's method for the temple was no different from that for his other houses. His 'plans' were usually general impressions of what the building would look like, without any technical indications. As he went along, he would work out the mathematics with his engineer and be incorporating new elements constantly. It was a costly and slow process, but one that allowed for improvisation and originality.

For many years, it was doubted that the Sagrada Família could be finished in line with Gaudí's ideas, especially since paperwork and models had been destroyed in 1936, but in the 1980s computer modelling was applied to Gaudí's designs. The computer programmer Mark Burry designed modelling techniques that showed how Gaudí's ideas could be completed. What Burry and his team found amazing was that Gaudí had been able to work out such complex three-dimensional designs.[10] His parents' workshop, where he watched sheets of metal transformed into three-dimensional objects, had formed his mind.

The Sagrada Família shows precisely how Gaudí's inspiration in nature was set in stone, as the architecture critic Jonathan Glancey explains:

> Gaudí based his designs on the complex forms we know today (or ought to know) as helicoids, hyperboloids and hyperbolic paraboloids. These are forms abstracted from nature and then translated into the design of the columns, vaults and intersecting geometric elements of the structure of the Sagrada Família.[11]

The Nativity facade has three portals, Hope, Charity and Faith. It was conceived as a giant Christmas crib or Nativity scene, its figures and scenes set in rocky, leaf-bound grottoes. It is divided into three parts, dedicated to Jesus and his parents Mary and Joseph and separated by two columns supported by the trumpeters announcing the Nativity. Facing the rising sun, it is an explosion of joy at God's nature bursting out at dawn and in spring.

The overall design and management of the building was the responsibility of Gaudí, but the work was done by a long team of

Sagrada Família. Nativity facade.

talented plasterers, stone-cutters and sculptors, first among them
Llorenç Matamala and later his son, Joan. Animals abound, as they
do in medieval cathedrals, making them attractive to the faithful:
dragonflies, an owl, a donkey, along with trees and flowers of all
kinds. Most figures also bear symbolic meanings: for example,
the cypress symbolizes eternal life; turtles, long life; white doves,
purity; the pelican, the Eucharist; bees, constant effort, and so forth.
Symbolism did not mean inattention to realist detail. Gaudí had a
live donkey hoisted up the facade, to see what a carving would look

like *in situ*. As he had done with Opisso and other victims, he then covered the donkey with plaster, left it to dry, then broke open the mould. Morbidly, he got hold of skeletons of people from a hospital to study bone structure, arranged to watch a patient die so that he could observe the exact moment the soul left the body, and in 1919 witnessed his friend and neighbour the medical student Alfonso Trias dissecting a corpse.[12] Like Dalí's Surrealist paintings, Gaudí's fantastic visions were based on hyper-realist detail.

Giralt-Miracle believes that the Sagrada Família concentrates 'all Gaudí's ideals (technical, artistic, patriotic and spiritual ideals) . . . the backbone of his creativity'.[13] Since he worked on it throughout his life, it integrates the advances he made at each stage of his architecture: ceramics in the Casa Vicens, arches and capture of light in the Teresianes, the internal spaces of the Casa Batlló, and the system of construction with catenary arches of the crypt at Santa Coloma that gave him the solution for the Sagrada Família.

David Mackay, in his thoughtful, carefully weighed words, praised 'Gaudí's personal style that gave a novel interpretation . . . to the Baroque'.[14] However, unlike Giralt-Miracle, Mackay sees the Sagrada Família not as the crowning climax of his career but rather as a decline as Gaudí 'withdrew more and more into his private obsessions':

> His abundant imagination, private wit and public self-confidence finally became mortgaged to a consuming and reactionary religiosity that grew up around him through his work on the Sagrada Família temple . . . His architecture became subjected to a religion of symbols.[15]

Arrest

Though Gaudí did not cede to urgings to join the Lliga or stand for office, as his fellow architects Domènech i Montaner and Puig i Cadafalch did, he regularly attended demonstrations for Catalan rights. In 1920 he was struck by police trying to clear the road after celebration of the *Jocs florals*. It appears that Gaudí, shouting

'Bloodthirsty pigs!' was only saved from further injury and arrest by two priests, who dragged him away.

In this time of acute class conflict, police commonly stopped and searched people in the street. Opisso told how one day, on stopping Gaudí, they asked: 'Are you carrying arms?' 'I certainly am,' he replied, and, at great risk of being shot, plunged his hands into his pockets and extracted various rosaries. 'These are my arms.'[16] Another anecdote of Gaudí's humour!

Each year, 11 September commemorates the fall of Barcelona to Philip v's troops in 1714, the defeat that led to fierce repression and suppression of Catalan institutions and language. General Primo de Rivera seized power in a military coup with the support of King Alfonso XIII on 13 September 1923, with the excuse of the large crowds that had demonstrated on 11 September shouting, *Visca Catalunya lliure!* (Long Live Free Catalonia!) and *Mori Espanya!* (Death to Spain!). Primo immediately banned the Catalan flag and any public use of Catalan.

The following year, on 11 September 1924, the first major commemoration of Catalan rights since Primo de Rivera's coup, Gaudí was about to enter the church of Sant Just near the cathedral for 8 a.m. Mass when he was stopped by the police. According to the police notes, a policeman tackled him in Castilian:

'Where are you going?'
'I'm going to Mass,' replied Gaudí in Catalan.
'You can't go in.'
'I'm going in.'

He was arrested. During the exchange in the police station, he was asked:

'Profession?'
'Architect.'
'Then your profession obliges you to talk in Castilian.'
'My profession obliges me to pay my taxes and I pay them, but not to stop speaking my own language.'[17]

From at least the turn of the century Gaudí refused to speak in Castilian Spanish. When the Basque writer and philosopher Miguel de Unamuno, not at all ill-disposed to Gaudí or to Catalonia, visited the Sagrada Família in 1906, the poet Joan Maragall had to translate Gaudí's explanations. On another occasion, he refused to speak Castilian to Alfonso XIII, forcing the Spanish prime minister Antonio Maura to break protocol and reply in Catalan (Maura spoke Catalan because he had been brought up in Mallorca). Gaudí of course understood and spoke Spanish perfectly: it was the language of his schooling. It was a political decision not to speak it.

The stubborn Catalan nationalist was fined 50 pesetas after this 1924 arrest and was locked up until he paid. He sent a message to a priest friend, who brought the money. Legend has it that he was in a cell with a migrant from another part of Spain, not a Catalan speaker, who had been fined 25 pesetas for illegally selling fruit in the street. Gaudí had asked his friend to bring 75 pesetas and paid the other man's fine, too. The grateful fruit seller asked for Gaudí's address so he could return the money, but Gaudí replied with haughty certainty: 'Charity is not to be returned.'[18] Gaudí enjoyed occupying the moral high ground.

The legend of Gaudí as the saintly architect of God is based on this final period, a legend that ignores his arrogance, his bad temper, his numerous conflicts with clients and his anticlericalism when young. The legend is what has enabled the Association for the Beatification of Antoni Gaudí, founded in 1992, to campaign for the *Architect of God*. The Church works slowly. The Vatican accepted the petition in 2000. The appropriate committee has spent years taking evidence and studying the case. It seems likely that within a few years he will become the 'Venerable' Antoni Gaudí, the step before sainthood.

The young architect Ernst Neufert (1900–1986) expressed the divine innocence of Gaudí after visiting him in his workshop in 1920 or 1921:

I saw there the ideal architect's workshop that Gropius had spoken of so much in the romantic beginnings of the Bauhaus.

There was the authentic Bauhütte, the cabin built on the firm
foundations of faith.[19]

The reaction of Neufert, follower and ally of Walter Gropius
(1883–1969), also shows how risky it is to separate styles too strictly
into *modernisme*, *noucentisme* or the modern movement. A central
Bauhaus concept was that buildings should combine all arts and
crafts, as in medieval cathedrals. What could be closer to Gaudí,
even as the Bauhaus rejected Gaudian baroque?

In early 1925, Gaudí wrote to the Archbishop of Tarragona to
leave some shares and a house he still owned in Riudoms (he was
not as poor as he appeared) to the Church. The shares were to pay
for a foundation to promote worship of the Virgin of Montserrat;
the house, to endow a foundation 'in loving memory of and prayer
for my Father'.[20]

The Tram

His worldly affairs settled, Gaudí took to sleeping on a cot in the
Sagrada Família workshop, an arrangement that became permanent
in 1925. This was due to his commitment to the temple but also
his love for Llorenç Matamala and Pere Santaló, who lived nearby.
Matamala, who had worked with Gaudí right from the start, was
dying of facial cancer. Gaudí visited him daily. He also visited each
evening his faithful friend Santaló, bedridden after a prostate
operation.

The stories of Antoni Gaudí's death have a legendary quality:
the ascetic, saintly old man building a medieval basilica is knocked
down by a twentieth-century tram. Just as there is doubt about
his birth (in Riudoms or Reus), so confusion surrounds his death.
Despite his fame, so ragged were his clothes and so worn his body
that he was mistaken for a pauper and was taken to the indigents'
ward. He was carrying no identity papers or money. Several taxis
refused to take him, owing to his apparent poverty,

Gaudí in his final years.

his underpants held together by safety-pins. His dishevelled, half-starved appearance, compounded by heavily bandaged knees as prevention against arthritic swelling, bedroom slippers and his baggy worn-out suit.[21]

The accident occurred on 7 June 1926, at the junction of the Gran Via and *carrer* Bailén. Gaudí, on his way to his daily devotions and confession at Sant Felip Neri, incautiously stepped off the pavement at about 5.30 p.m. Or maybe it wasn't lack of caution. Gaudí believed pedestrians should have priority over cars and trams (one of his more logical opinions). He told Cèsar Martinell that one evening he refused to react to a tram driver's frequent blasts on the horn, forcing the driver to brake sharply. The driver leaped down from the tram, remonstrated with Gaudí and threw sand in his face. If on 7 June he stepped off the pavement deliberately, Gaudí may have died as he lived: in cussed obstinacy.

The unlucky tram driver told the press that the tramp was 'undoubtedly' drunk. Unfortunately for the driver, the 'tramp' never touched alcohol. When he failed to return to the Sagrada Família that night, the caretakers advised Domènec Sugranyes, who finally tracked Gaudí down in the Santes Creus hospital. The moneyless and paperless tramp had been diagnosed with broken ribs and a brain haemorrhage. Sugranyes had him transferred from the poor ward to a private room. Gaudí asked for and received the last rites. The consternation that the news of his injury caused in Barcelona underlined his fame, however much he had been mocked. Bishops, architects (Puig i Cadafalch, Jujol) and politicians (Francesc Cambó, leader of the Lliga) jostled in the hospital's corridors. The city mayor offered to transfer him to a luxurious private clinic, but Gaudí refused.

Gaudí died three days after his accident, at 5 p.m. on Thursday 10 June. Joan Matamala, son of Llorenç and likewise a sculptor on the Sagrada Família, took a death mask. The funeral procession on Saturday 12 June drew enormous crowds, who applauded on the pavements and followed the dignitaries behind the horse-drawn hearse. Black ribbons hung from many balconies. There had not been such a mass funeral since that of his friend Jacint Verdaguer, who by one of those strange twists of fate died on exactly the same date 24 years earlier. There would not be another funeral procession so great until that of the anarchist leader Buenaventura Durruti on 23 November 1936. Deeply pessimistic about Primo de Rivera's anti-Catalanist dictatorship, Gaudí had told Martinell: 'We are stuck in a cul-de-sac . . . A radical change must definitely come.'[22] Durruti represented this radical change. However, Durruti's revolution was the revolutionary change that Gaudí feared and abhorred, not the Catholic Catalanist purification that Gaudí desired.

Special papal dispensation was obtained for Gaudí's burial in the crypt of the Sagrada Família.

10

Gaudí after Death

In the mid-1980s, when I first saw the Casa Milà, it was in a bad way. The facade was black with the city's soot.[1] The top floor had been converted into thirteen flats. The wonderful frescoes and the paintings flowing along the ceilings of the public spaces were cracked and discoloured. The mosaic was chipped.

The Caixa Catalunya savings bank bought the house in 1986, and by 1993 it had been returned to its original glory, with no less a person supervising the fresco work than Gianluigi Colalucci (1929–2021), restorer of the ceiling of the Vatican's Sistine Chapel. The Casa Milà's rebirth is very much part of the take-off of Barcelona as a great art tourism destination, starting in the mid-1980s when the 1992 Olympic Games were awarded to the city. The Olympics were the catalyst for the overhaul and reform of the dirty, neglected city of the Franco dictatorship. The City Council was firmly set on developing tourism as industry declined. Gaudí was the centrepiece of this project.

Reputation

Gaudí's legacy has been strange and contradictory. Gaudí is now Barcelona's main tourist attraction, boosted by International Gaudí Year in 2002, when over twenty exhibitions were promoted in the city, numerous books were published and discounts offered on entry to houses. That year saw tourism to the city increase dramatically, with visits to the Sagrada Família and Gaudí houses the main attraction. Since then, tourism to Barcelona and visits to

Gaudí buildings have continued to rise.[2] Queues were common. To avoid them, most houses and the basilica now require advance booking online.

This is a remarkable turnaround, as Gaudí's reputation, already low in his last years, plummeted after his death. The younger architects of the GATCPAC were respectful of his structures but turned their backs on what they saw as his old-fashioned, fanciful work;[3] for Josep Lluís Sert and the 'modern movement', Gaudí was a one-off dead end. Work on the Sagrada Família continued to limp, then stopped totally between the outbreak of the Civil War in 1936 and 1952. However, there have always been ardent Catholic Catalanist supporters of Gaudí, and they, led by Domènec Sugranyes, completed the towers of the Nativity façade by 1930.

The other group that promoted Gaudí in the decades after his death were the absolute antithesis to these faithful Catholics: the Surrealists, who saw his buildings as projections of dreams. Man Ray visited Barcelona in 1933 and photographed Gaudí buildings. These accompanied an influential article by Dalí in the Parisian magazine *Minotaure*, entitled 'On the Terrifying and Edible Beauty of the Modern Style'.[4] Dora Maar, Marcel Duchamp and Paul Éluard all praised Gaudí's work as surrealist, though clearly the architect himself had nothing in common with the anti-family, anti-Church and anti-capitalist ideals of the Surrealist movement. In 1936, the Museum of Modern Art in New York included Gaudí in its exhibition *Fantastic Art, Dada, Surrealism*.

The architects who followed Gaudí did not imitate him, but the idea, common a few decades ago, that he was an isolated, ignored genius is unsustainable. Both in his lifetime and afterwards, the world's leading architects openly admired him. Le Corbusier (1887–1965), in many ways the anti-Gaudí with his straight lines, utilitarian blocks and use of unadorned concrete, nevertheless affirmed on visits to Barcelona that Gaudí was 'a man of extraordinary force, faith and technical skill . . . Only those who touch men's sensitive hearts will last . . . even though they are mistreated along the way.'[5] And several critics have noted the debt of Le Corbusier's Ronchamp chapel to Gaudí's crypt at Santa Coloma.

The North American architect of skyscrapers Louis Sullivan (1856–1924) defined the Sagrada Família as 'spirit symbolized in stone', and Walter Gropius praised Gaudí's 'technical perfection'.[6] The previous chapter touched on how Gropius's Bauhaus and Gaudí shared an emphasis on artisan methods.

Two modern architects of renown claim Gaudí's heritage. The Valencian Santiago Calatrava (b. 1951) wrote:

> People have tried to understand Gaudí in terms of paganism, masonry, Buddhism or atheism. I believe that he was a man who served a religious idea, but the god, or rather the goddess that Gaudí revered was Architecture itself.[7]

Calatrava's soaring bridges do not obviously make one think of Gaudí. Yet Calatrava also tends to talk in terms of nature, of creating twisting shapes that imitate nature. For instance, his unfinished Dubai Creek Tower 'is inspired by the delicate veins of lily leaves'.[8]

The other great architect inspired by Gaudí is the Catalan Enric Miralles (1955–2000). Professor Carolina García Estévez told me a magnificent story. In the forest (before the trees were chopped down) around Gaudí's unfinished chapel at the Colònia Güell, basalt columns, so hard to carve or smooth, were left lying on the ground. When one of the steel hawsers for the roof of Miralles's gymnasium at Huesca snapped at Easter 1993 because it had been attached wrongly, he remembered those columns abandoned in the undergrowth:

> With the romantic vision of the basalt columns of the Güell crypt, Miralles decided to leave the two broken hawsers on the ground, as a sign of the passage of time and the inexorable failure of architecture before time. He then projected a new roof that didn't require hawsers.[9]

Gaudí's influence may not be obvious or direct, but he created an echo that subsequent architects like Miralles hear. Rather than a style, this is a general, intangible influence: his triumph

The Passage of Time. Enric Miralles at the Güell crypt.

of individualism and the quixotic over cold, uniform corporate architecture liberated architects.

Mackay argues that Catalan art nouveau had a strong popular influence, unlike art nouveau in the other countries where it flourished as architecture. Although there is no clear line from Gaudí to later architects, no school of Gaudí, *modernisme* did enter popular culture. It became not just an extravagant museum piece but part of vernacular architecture in subsequent generations. If you stroll round the outlying suburbs of Barcelona, you often find houses with *modernista* touches: a curving line here, stone-carved grapes there. His influence freed people from dependence on the straight line. Though these touches are in general surface additions to a conventional structure, they show that Gaudí and art nouveau left their marks on popular taste.

In the Civil War, his Sagrada Família workshop was trashed (in the anarchist revolution he so feared) and his plans were lost. The Left had always been hostile to Gaudí for ideological reasons: after all, his life's work was to win workers from anarchism to religion. Often this blinded leftists to the revolutionary nature of his architecture. In his paean to the anarchist Barcelona of 1917, the Russian revolutionary Victor Serge wrote:

> The four towers of the Holy Family, held aloft by intricate scaffolding, extend their apocalyptic ugliness into the blue. They look like monumental factory chimneys, only misshapen, crying out their uselessness.[10]

And here is the equally philistine attitude of George Orwell in 1936:

> I went to have a look at the cathedral – a modern cathedral, and one of the most hideous buildings in the world. It has four crenellated spires exactly the shape of hock bottles . . . I think the Anarchists showed bad taste in not blowing it up . . . though they did hang a red and black banner between its spires.[11]

Criticism was not just from foreigners. In the oppressive atmosphere of the 1940s, after Franco's Civil War victory, few in Catalonia and Spain were in favour of continuing work on the temple. There was no money; and further, Gaudí's Catalanism did not endear him or his works to the centralist, Spanish-nationalist dictatorship. And for a left-wing art critic, Gaya Nuño, imprisoned by Franco, Gaudí's works were 'abortions in stone' and 'obscene bulbs' produced by 'tortured imagination'.[12]

House in Horta, Barcelona. Example of a vernacular *modernista* style.

Traditionally, the Left has been against the basilica, mixing political (the Church is repressive), social (build housing, not churches) and artistic (it's ugly) criteria. Though the American novelist Barbara Wilson expressed ambivalence, not outright rejection, in *Gaudí Afternoon* (1990), her narrator Cassandra put one political argument clearly:

> Sagrada Família . . . was meant to symbolize the stability and order of family life. Perhaps that was what gave me such a queasy

sensation . . . it was monumentally, phenomenally bizarre, like
the Christian notion of family itself, a combination of organic
and tortured form.[13]

Renewal

The Sagrada Família's construction started again in 1952, with
the foundations of the Passion facade facing west. Now a Franco
supporter, Dalí continued to praise Gaudí as he had done in
the 1930s. The architect's reputation began to rise. In 1957 the
Museum of Modern Art organized a major Gaudí exhibition in
New York. Pevsner had omitted Gaudí from his 1936 *Pioneers
of Modern Design,* but in later editions devoted several pages to
praising Gaudí's 'intrepid daring' and the Sagrada Família's spires'
'amazing pattern of voids and solids and their even more amazing
crustacean pinnacles'.[14]

The political changes and cultural earthquakes of the 1960s
created new admirers of Gaudí. Mass tourism reached Spain.
Japanese tourists, in particular, began to visit and donate money
to the Sagrada Família, accelerating work. The cultural revolution
of the 1960s brought a new eye to the curves and baroque
exaggerations of Gaudí's buildings. Hippies could lie around
smoking dope in the free-entry, municipally run Park Güell and
confuse Gaudí's toadstools with Timothy Leary's magic mushrooms.

Catalonia is a country of great twentieth-century visual artists,
such as Miró, Dalí, Julio González, Remedios Varo, Picasso and
Antoni Tàpies, but Gaudí towers above them (even Picasso) as a
tourist attraction. His very name is used to add value: to restaurants,
hotels, estate agents, trinkets, toys, annual cinema awards,
Barcelona fashion week and more. In the Casa Milà shop you can
buy Gaudí cups, plates, mats, bags, T-shirts, bookmarks, chairs,
pencils, notebooks and even a small colourful plastic bottle of *Aigua
La Pedrera,* 'The Best Water to Remember'.

The 2002 Gaudí Year saw the Catalan government and Barcelona
City Council investing in Gaudí buildings and exhibitions. In
the twenty-first century the Sagrada Família's construction has

moved ahead faster. Pope Benedict xvi consecrated the main church on 7 November 2010. It is no coincidence that the date was the anniversary of the Russian Revolution: the basilica's backers and builders are still active warriors against anarchism and communism. The pope said: 'Gaudí with his work shows us that God is the true measure of man. That the secret of genuine originality lies in returning to the origin, which is God.'

Until the Covid-19 pandemic, the building was financed by the 2.5 million visitors a year who paid between 17 and 32 euros per person for entry. These are not exactly donations, as was the original idea, but it does mean that neither Church nor state is paying for the temple. It is now the most visited tourist site in the Spanish state, ahead of Madrid's Prado Museum or Granada's Alhambra.[15] The Sagrada Família has become the symbol of Barcelona, just as the Eiffel Tower is of Paris.

Gaudí tourist tat.

Awfulness beyond Description

Many believe it should have been left unfinished. On 9 January 1965, twenty architects and artists signed a letter against its continuation. These included Le Corbusier, Pevsner, the painter Miró and Oriol Bohigas (1925–2021), the main architect and town planner in Barcelona's urban regeneration from the early 1980s on. Josep Maria Subirachs (1927–2014) was also a signatory, but he had changed his mind by June 1986, when he accepted the commission to carve fourteen sculptures on the Passion facade. The letter argued that there were no social, urban design, religious or artistic justifications for continuing work on the basilica.[16]

Supporters of completing the basilica point to the long decades and centuries that construction of medieval cathedrals took. Many, who may favour continuing work to finish the basilica, abhor Subirachs's work. The critic Rowan Moore wrote in 2011 that 'the Passion Facade, a grim counterpart to the lush Nativity Facade . . . has sculptures of cartoonish anguish by artist Josep María Subirachs, the awfulness of which is beyond description.'[17] Public polemic delighted press and television, as Subirachs waded into his critics as 'hooligans, snobs – a Mafia of colleagues jealous that they weren't hired for the job'.[18]

In nearly twenty years, Subirachs carved one hundred stone figures and made four vast bronze doors for the basilica's west facade. In 1990, many Catalan artists organized a demonstration against his angular 'distortion' of Gaudí.[19] This missed the point: Subirachs never pretended to be imitating Gaudí. His execution can be seen as deficient or not: this is subjective. However, his expressionist style of rough-surfaced, sharp-angled and anguished figures is in line with Gaudí's stated desire for harsh and cruel imagery on the Passion facade.

In October 2018, the construction board was finally granted a building permit by the City Council. Gaudí had always been one to go ahead now and face down the council later. In this case, when the village of Sant Martí de Provençals, to which the Sagrada Família site originally belonged, was incorporated into Barcelona in 1897,

Basilica among the houses. Glory facade, Sagrada Família.

no new permit had been applied for. Under the 2018 agreement, the underground station will have a direct entrance to the temple and the construction board agrees to pay €36 million to neighbourhood persons and entities in compensation for all the trouble caused to the

Protest. 'Thou shall not covet the goods of others.'

area. These include taxi and coach jams, local food shops converted to bars and restaurants, a constant market selling souvenirs, masses of photographers blocking pavements and so on. A further nightmare for residents of the block facing the still-to-be-completed facade of Glory on *carrer* Mallorca is the proposal of the construction board to demolish the whole block. The idea, opposed by the City Council, is to extend stairs or a ramp over *carrer* Mallorca from the facade of Glory. This is the ugly side of the Church's tourism industry. Never has an unfinished building been so successful.

The passion for Gaudí does not only involve the Sagrada Família. The Park Güell, the Casa Batlló and the Casa Milà all have to be pre-booked unless you want to queue to visit. Other houses (the Casa Vicens, Bellesguard) have been bought by banks, which have opened their doors to the public. There is money in the passion for Gaudí; and banks purchase goodwill by associating themselves with art.

Who knows what Gaudí would have thought of it all? He would have taken reverence and admiration of his talent as his due, for he knew he was a great architect. And he would have fulminated against the irreligious, money-making mass consumption of tourism today, for he was both an awkward character and authentically austere.

References

Introduction

1 UNESCO, World Heritage Convention, https://whc.unesco.org/en/
   list/320, accessed 20 June 2023.

1 Watching Nature Twist and Turn

1 Letter of resignation of King Amadeo to the Spanish Congress, 11
   February 1873, https://es.wikipedia.org/wiki/Amadeo_I_de_España,
   accessed 20 June 2023.
2 Richard Ford, *Handbook for Spain 1845* (Arundel, 1966), vol. II, p. 712.
3 J. Castellar-Gassol, *The Life of a Visionary* (Barcelona, 2015), p. 25.
4 Ibid., p. 31.
5 Ibid., p. 32.
6 The medieval Crown of Aragon included Aragon, Catalonia and
   Valencia. Its monarch was most usually known as the Count of
   Barcelona.
7 Rose Macaulay, *Fabled Shore* (London, 1949), p. 73.
8 Robert Hughes, *Barcelona* (London, 1992), p. 472.
9 Gijs van Hensbergen, *Gaudí* (London, 2002), p. 18. The quote within
   the quote comes from an 1878 comment by Gaudí.
10 Van Hensbergen, ibid., pp. 26 and 31–2, gives these addresses.
11 Ibid., p. 31.
12 Hughes, *Barcelona*, p. 357.
13 The manuscript was almost unknown until 1967, when the architect
   Cèsar Martinell (1888–1975) discovered it in the Reus County Museum
   (Museu Comarcal Salvador Vilaseca, Reus – www.museudereus.cat),
   where Sugranyes had deposited it in the 1930s.

14 Hughes, *Barcelona*, p. 480.

15 Panot tiles are decorative paving tiles for indoor and outdoor use. See Stephen Burgen, 'A Man on a Mission to Preserve Barcelona's Decorative Floor Tiles', *The Guardian*, 10 January 2022.

16 Elies Rogent's comment is echoed in Jack Nicholson's question to the architecture student played by Maria Schneider in Michelangelo Antonioni's *The Passenger* (1975): 'D'you think he was crazy?'

2 Influences

1 *La maquinista* was something of an exception. What is often called the second stage of the Industrial Revolution, in which heavy industry replaced textiles, was stunted in Catalonia and the Spanish state.

2 Arthur Terry, *A Literary History of Spain: Catalan Literature* (London, 1972), p. 75.

3 Gijs van Hensbergen, *Gaudí* (London, 2002), p. 49. The translated text does not fully follow Van Hensbergen's translation. The original 'La casa pairal', part of the Manuscript of Reus, can be found online: see www.casavicens.org.

4 Nikolaus Pevsner in John Fleming et al., *The Penguin Dictionary of Architecture* (London, 1972), p. 301.

5 Juan José Lahuerta, *Antoni Gaudí: Ornament, Fire and Ashes* (Barcelona, 2016), p. 14. Lahuerta is the holder of the Càtedra Gaudí (Chair in Gaudí Studies) at the ETSAB (Escola Tècnica Superior d'Arquitectura de Barcelona) and the author of several books on Gaudí. He was curator of the huge 2022 *Gaudí* exhibition at the Museu Nacional d'Art de Catalunya in Barcelona and the Musée d'Orsay and Musée de l'Orangerie in Paris.

6 Ibid., p. 14.

7 José Ràfols, *Antonio Gaudí* (Barcelona, 1949), p. 26.

8 The ETSAB library today holds the translation of Owen Jones's *Plans, Elevations, Sections and Details of the Alhambra* that Gaudí used (with his annotations) to understand the ornamentation of the Alhambra Palace in Granada and the origin of its forms in nature.

9 John Ruskin, *The Study of Architecture in Our Schools* (1865), cited in James Dearden, *John Ruskin* (Kettering, n.d.), p. 14.

10 Lahuerta, *Ornament, Fire and Ashes*, p. 24.

11 Marilyn McCully, ed., *Homage to Barcelona: The City and Its Art, 1888–1936* (London, 1986), Introduction, p. 17.
12 Robert Hughes, *Barcelona* (London, 1992), p. 479.

3 The Free-Thinking Family

1 Letter quoted in Rainer Zerbst, *Antoni Gaudí* (Cologne, 1989), p. 21.
2 Gijs van Hensbergen, *Gaudí* (London, 2002), p. 54. Gaudí had not been looking at the clouds on a dull winter's day when he wrote this in the unpublished 'Notes on Ornamentation' (part of the Reus Manuscript).
3 Ibid., p. 55.
4 Robert Hughes, *Barcelona* (London, 1992), p. 477.
5 Ibid., p. 476.
6 Josep Pla, 'Antoni Gaudí', in *Alguns homenots* (Barcelona, 1991), p. 13. The ironic and playful Josep Pla (1897–1981), one of Catalonia's most celebrated writers, knew many people who had known Gaudí.
7 Ibid.
8 J. Castellar-Gassol, *Gaudí: The Life of a Visionary* (Barcelona, 2015), p. 85.
9 Ibid., p. 68.
10 Ibid., p. 69.
11 Hughes, *Barcelona*, p. 475. If not always accurate, Hughes is often worth quoting for the exuberance of his language, which catches the beauty of the buildings.
12 Ibid., p. 478.
13 Pla, 'Antoni Gaudí', p. 18.
14 Ibid., pp. 21–2.

4 The First Great Houses

1 Daniel Giralt-Miracle, *Gaudí essencial* (Barcelona, 2012), pp. 175–6.
2 The Casa Vicens is one of Gaudí's best-known but least seen buildings, as it was not opened to the public until November 2017. It was in private hands (though no longer the Vicens family's) until 2014, when it was bought by the Andorran bankers MoraBanc and refurbished.
3 Joan Bergós, *Gaudí: L'home i l'obra* (Barcelona, 1999), p. 53.
4 David Mackay, *Modern Architecture in Barcelona, 1854–1939* (Sheffield, 1985), p. 12. David Mackay (1933–2014) was one of Barcelona's most

prominent architects, a member of the MBM partnership from 1962 until his death.

5   Nikolaus Pevsner in John Fleming et al., *The Penguin Dictionary of Architecture* (London, 1972), p. 113.

6   Gijs van Hensbergen, *Gaudí* (London, 2002), p. 79.

7   Joan Bassegoda, *Gaudí: Arquitectura del futuro* (Barcelona, 1984), p. 24.

8   Felicitously, a full-scale facsimile of the cascade from the garden of the Casa Vicens, 10 × 10 metres (33 × 33 ft) of beautiful artisan-made brick, was built in the gardens of the Museu de les Aigües (Water Museum) at Cornellà, near Barcelona, and opened to the public in April 2019.

9   Bergós, *Gaudí: L'home i l'obra*, p. 53. Quijano is the 'real' name of Don Quijote in Cervantes's novel.

10 Rainer Zerbst, *Antoni Gaudí: A Life Devoted to Architecture* (London, 1985), p. 48.

11 Ibid., p. 48.

12 David Mackay, *Modern Architecture in Barcelona*, p. 18.

13 Bassegoda, *Gaudí: Arquitectura del futuro*, pp. 10 and 125.

14 Van Hensbergen, *Gaudí*, p. 63.

15 Ibid., p. 64.

16 Robert Hughes, *Barcelona* (London, 1992), p. 483.

17 Pevsner in Fleming et al., *Penguin Dictionary of Architecture*, p. 113.

18 Juan José Lahuerta, *Antoni Gaudí: Ornament, Fire and Ashes* (Barcelona, 2016), p. 37.

19 Ibid., p. 37.

20 Today, the stables house the library of the Chair in Gaudí Studies (Càtedra Gaudí).

21 It is often said that Gaudí created no school of architects. However, this does not mean he had no influence on architects or on fashion (see Chapter Ten). Rainer Zerbst (*Antoni Gaudí*, p. 76) writes that these doors caused a sensation. They were at first ridiculed but were then imitated.

22 Alastair Boyd, *The Essence of Catalonia* (London, 1988), p. 250.

23 Juan-Eduardo Cirlot, *Gaudí: An Introduction to His Architecture*, trans. Steve Cedar (Barcelona, 2001), p. 47.

24 Mackay, *Modern Architecture in Barcelona*, pp. 21–2.

25 Interview with Professor Carolina García Estévez, 11 February 2020.

26 Zerbst, *Antoni Gaudí*, p. 70.

27 Cristina Mendoza and Eduardo Mendoza, *Barcelona modernista* (Barcelona, 1989), p. 84.

28 Hughes, *Barcelona*, p. 497.

29 Colm Tóibín, *Homage to Barcelona* (London, 1994), p. 72.

5 Religious Crisis

1 David Mackay, 'Searching for a New Language in the Past', in *Barcelona: Metròpolis mediterrània*, 58 (2002).
2 Gijs van Hensbergen, *Gaudí* (London, 2002), p. 106.
3 Jaume Crosas, *Gaudí: El seu temps i la seva obra* (Terrassa, 1986), p. 44.
4 Joan Bergós, *Gaudí: L'home i l'obra* (Barcelona, 1999), p. 31.
5 Van Hensbergen, *Gaudí*, p. 101.
6 Jan Morris, *Spain* (London, 2008), p. 64.
7 Bergós, *Gaudí: L'home i l'obra*, p. 126.
8 Van Hensbergen, *Gaudí*, p. 104.
9 Bergós, *Gaudí: L'home i l'obra*, p. 57.
10 J. Castellar-Gassol, *Gaudí: The Life of a Visionary* (Barcelona, 2015), p. 73.
11 Bergós, *Gaudí: L'home i l'obra*, p. 45.
12 Colm Tóibín, *Homage to Barcelona* (London, 1994), p. 73.
13 Bergós, *Gaudí: L'home i l'obra*, p. 42.

6 The Spoiled Child of the Industrial Revolution

1 I have used these two terms, *modernisme* and art nouveau, interchangeably throughout the book.
2 Nikolaus Pevsner, *Pioneers of Modern Design* (London, 1970), p. 110.
3 This essay is discussed in detail in Juan José Lahuerta, *Antoni Gaudí: Ornament, Fire and Ashes* (Barcelona, 2016), Chapter One. Also cited in Gijs van Hensbergen, *Gaudí* (London, 2002), pp. 54–5.
4 Ignasi de Solà-Morales, 'Modernista Architecture', in *Homage to Barcelona: The City and Its Art, 1888–1936* , ed. Marilyn McCully (London, 1986), p. 124. Solà-Morales is the grandson of Gaudí's close collaborator Joan Rubió.
5 Richard Burton, *Prague: A Cultural and Literary History* (Oxford, 2003), p. 137.
6 Michael Jacobs, *Barcelona* (Blue Guide) (London, 1991), p. 128. The building, reformed in the 1980s, is now the Antoni Tàpies Foundation, at *carrer* Aragó 255.
7 Van Hensbergen, *Gaudí*, p. 222.
8 Robert Hughes, *Barcelona* (London, 1992), pp. 401–2.
9 Els Quatre Gats is still there, restored to how it was in 1897–1903. In Catalan, *quatre gats* (literally, four cats) means 'hardly anyone', the equivalent to the English term 'three men and a dog'.

10 Michael Eaude, *Catalonia: A Cultural History* (Oxford, 2007), p. 110.
11 Daniel Giralt-Miracle, *Gaudí essencial* (Barcelona, 2012), p. 180.
12 Hughes, *Barcelona*, pp. 317–18.
13 Torras i Bages's book *La tradició catalana* is discussed in Jaume Crosas, *Gaudí: El seu temps i la seva obra* (Terrassa, 1986), pp. 17–18, and Hughes, *Barcelona*, pp. 319–20.
14 Eliseu Trenc Ballester and Alan Yates, *Alexandre de Riquer* (Sheffield, 1988), p. 15.
15 Eaude, *Catalonia*, p. 97.
16 Oriol Bohigas, 'Gaudí, entre Rusiñol y Dalí', *El País*, 8 January 2003.

7 The Busy Years

1 Gijs van Hensbergen, *Gaudí* (London, 2002), p. 157.
2 Ibid., pp. 121–2.
3 Readers have narrowly missed out on the opportunity of a really solid Gaudí souvenir. The bottom half of the Casa Clapés, on the market for several years for €1.8 million, was sold in 2022 for an undisclosed sum.
4 Gaudi's well-known abstemious habits did not prevent the philosopher Miguel de Unamuno from finding him guilty of 'drunken architecture'.
5 Daniel Giralt-Miracle, *Gaudí essencial* (Barcelona, 2012), p. 136.
6 Rainer Zerbst, *Antoni Gaudí: A Life Devoted to Architecture* (London, 1985), p. 231.
7 Ibid., p. 106.
8 Isabel López had a somewhat prickly relationship with the brusque Gaudí, who spent vast amounts of her husband's money. Not to be confused with Isabel Güell, who was Isabel López and Eusebi Güell's oldest daughter. Isabel Güell, it appears, had a friendly, easy relationship with Gaudí.
9 Zerbst, *Antoni Gaudí*, p. 102.
10 Joan Bergós, *Gaudí: L'home i l'obra* (Barcelona, 1999), p. 148.
11 Zerbst, *Antoni Gaudí*, p. 218.
12 Nikolaus Pevsner in John Fleming et al., *The Penguin Dictionary of Architecture* (London, 1972), p. 113.
13 Interview with Julio Cortázar in the programme 'A Fondo', Spanish Television (TVE), 20 March 1977. Available on www.rtve.es/play/internacional/portada, accessed 20 June 2023.
14 Güell's old factory, El Vapor Vell, has been beautifully reconstructed as the Sants public library.

15 Joan Matamala says Gaudí's towers would have reached 360 metres (1,180 ft), higher than the then unbuilt Empire State Building.
16 Bergós, *Gaudí: L'home i l'obra*, p. 62.
17 Robert Hughes, *Barcelona* (London, 1992), p. 502.
18 Van Hensbergen, *Gaudí*, p. 140.
19 Hughes, *Barcelona*, p. 501.
20 Alastair Boyd, *The Essence of Catalonia* (London, 1988), p. 202.
21 Nikolaus Pevsner, *Pioneers of Modern Design* (London, 1970), p. 112.

8 Everything Flows

1 Eduardo Mendoza and Cristina Mendoza, *Barcelona modernista* (Barcelona, 1989), p. 9.
2 Gijs van Hensbergen, *Gaudí* (London, 2002), p. 138.
3 David Mackay, *Modern Architecture in Barcelona, 1854–1939* (Sheffield, 1985), p. 34.
4 Rainer Zerbst, *Antoni Gaudí: A Life Devoted to Architecture* (London, 1985), p. 160.
5 Maria Antonietta Crippa, *Antoni Gaudí, 1852–1926: From Nature to Architecture* (London, 2015), p. 6.
6 Robert Hughes, *Barcelona* (London, 1992), p. 513.
7 Juan José Lahuerta comments extensively on reactions to Gaudí in his years of fame in *Antoni Gaudí: Ornament, Fire and Ashes* (Barcelona, 2016), pp. 82–116, and on the Casa Batlló in particular on p. 113. See also Van Hensbergen, *Gaudí*, pp. 176–80.
8 Colm Tóibín, *Homage to Barcelona* (London, 1994), p. 75.
9 Mackay, *Modern Architecture in Barcelona*, p. 29.
10 Hughes, *Barcelona*, p. 516.
11 Van Hensbergen, *Gaudí*, p. 165.
12 Ibid., p. 174.
13 Robert Hughes, 'A Hulking, Delirious Beauty', *The Guardian*, 10 October 2007.
14 Zerbst, *Antoni Gaudí*, p. 176.
15 Vanessa Graell, 'El modernismo surrealista de Jujol', *El Mundo*, 14 February 2014.
16 Hughes, 'A Hulking, Delirious Beauty'.
17 Van Hensbergen, *Gaudí*, p. 174.
18 Ibid., p. 245.
19 Nikolaus Pevsner, *Pioneers of Modern Design* (London, 1970), p. 116.

9 Stubborn as a Pig

1 All quotes in this paragraph are from Josep Pla, 'Antoni Gaudí', in *Alguns homenots* (Barcelona, 1991), pp. 52–7. See also Gijs van Hensbergen, *Gaudí* (London, 2002), pp. 223–5.
2 Joan Bergós, *Gaudí: L'home i l'obra* (Barcelona, 1999), p. 56.
3 Ibid., pp. 45–6.
4 Maria Antonietta Crippa, *Antoni Gaudí, 1852–1926: From Nature to Architecture* (London, 2015), p. 10.
5 Pla, 'Antoni Gaudí', p. 45.
6 Ibid., p. 37.
7 Ibid., p. 36.
8 Cèsar Martinell quoted in Pla, 'Antoni Gaudí', p. 50.
9 Bergós, *Gaudí: L'home i l'obra*, p. 70.
10 Jonathan Glancey, 'Gaudí's La Sagrada Família: Genius or Folly', BBC Culture, www.bbc.com, 21 October 2014.
11 Ibid.
12 Gijs van Hensbergen, *Gaudí* (London, 2002), pp. 255–6.
13 Daniel Giralt-Miracle, *Gaudí essencial* (Barcelona, 2012), p. 176.
14 David Mackay, *Modern Architecture in Barcelona, 1854–1939* (Sheffield, 1985), pp. 24–30.
15 Ibid., p. 30.
16 Víctor Fernández, 'Ricardo Opisso, el hombre que lo sabía todo sobre Gaudí', *La Razón*, 6 January 2021.
17 César Martinell, *Gaudí: Su vida, su teoría, su obra* (Barcelona, 1967), pp. 105–7; Van Hensbergen, *Gaudí*, pp. 259–60.
18 J. Castellar-Gassol, *Gaudí: The Life of a Visionary* (Barcelona, 2015), pp. 115–17.
19 Ernst Neufert quoted ibid., p. 111.
20 Ibid., p. 117.
21 Van Hensbergen, *Gaudí*, p. 263.
22 Ibid., p. 260.

10 Gaudí after Death

1 Antonioni's *The Passenger* shows the same filthy exterior, from 1975.
2 Trends and figures sourced from Ana M. López, 'Tourism in Barcelona: Statistics and Facts', www.statista.com, 8 May 2023.

3 The GATCPAC (Group of Catalan Artists and Technicians for Progress in Contemporary Architecture) was a group of influential Catalan architects around Josep Lluís Sert in the 1930s. They were more socially progressive than their hero Le Corbusier.
4 Salvador Dalí, 'De la beauté terrifiante et comestible de l'architecture Modern'style', *Minotaure*, 3–4 (December 1933), pp. 69–76.
5 Claudia Vargas, *Antoni Gaudí: La arquitectura de la naturaleza* (Bogotá, 2004), pp. 72–3.
6 Jonathan Glancey, 'Gaudí's La Sagrada Família: Genius or Folly', BBC Culture, www.bbc.com, 21 October 2014.
7 Vargas, *Antoni Gaudí*, pp. 73–4.
8 Michael Eaude, *Sails and Winds* (Oxford, 2019), p. 194.
9 Interview with Carolina García Estévez, 11 February 2020.
10 Victor Serge, *Birth of Our Power* (London, 1977), p. 108.
11 George Orwell, *Homage to Catalonia* (London, 1970), original Chapter Fourteen. Though Orwell says 'cathedral', he is referring to the basilica.
12 Daniel Giralt-Miracle, Introduction to Joan Bergós, *Gaudí: L'home i l'obra* (Barcelona, 1999), p. 9.
13 Barbara Wilson, *Gaudí Afternoon* (London, 1991), p. 81.
14 Nikolaus Pevsner, *Pioneers of Modern Design* (London, 1970), p. 116.
15 In 2022, the Sagrada Família received 3,781,845 visitors; Madrid's Prado Museum, 2,456,724; and the Alhambra in Granada, 2,385,461. Figures are from the UNWTO (World Tourism Organization), cited in www.expansion.com, accessed 25 June 2023. A decade earlier the Alhambra had been the most visited tourism site in Spain.
16 The protest letter was published in *La Vanguardia* on 9 January 1965.
17 Rowan Moore, 'Sagrada Família: Gaudí's Cathedral Is Nearly Done, but Would He Have Liked It?' *The Observer*, 24 April 2011.
18 Margot Hornblower, 'My Client Isn't in Any Hurry', *Time*, 19 November 1990, pp. 64–5.
19 Lourdes Morgades, 'La Sagrada Família de la discordia', *El País*, 8 July 1990.

Select Bibliography

Part One: Books about Gaudí

Bassegoda, Juan, *Gaudí: arquitectura del futuro* (Barcelona, 1984); translated
  as *Gaudí: Master Architect* (New York, 2000)
Bergós, Joan, *Gaudí: L'home i l'obra* (Barcelona, 1999)
Castellar-Gassol, J., *Gaudí: The Life of a Visionary* (Barcelona, 2015)
Cirlot, Juan-Eduardo, *Gaudí. An Introduction to His Architecture,* trans. Steve
  Cedar (Barcelona, 2001)
Crippa, Maria Antonietta, *Antoni Gaudi, 1952–1926: From Nature to
  Architecture,* trans. Jeremy Carden (London, 2015)
Crosas, Jaume, *Gaudí: El seu temps i la seva obra* (Terrassa, 1986)
Dos de Arte Ediciones, ed., *Antoni Gaudí* (Barcelona, 2011)
Fontbona, Francesc, *Gaudí al detall* (Barcelona, 2002)
Giralt-Miracle, Daniel, *Gaudí essencial* (Barcelona, 2012)
van Hensbergen, Gijs, *Gaudí* (London, 2002)
Lahuerta, Juan José, *Antoni Gaudí: Ornament, Fire and Ashes,* trans. Graham
  Thomson (Barcelona, 2016)
Martinell, César, *Gaudí: su vida, su teoría, su obra* (Barcelona, 1967)
Pla, Josep, 'Antoni Gaudí', in *Alguns homenots* (Barcelona, 1991), pp. 11–58
Ràfols, José F., *Antonio Gaudí* (Barcelona, 1949)
Roe, Jeremy, *Antoni Gaudí: Architect and Artist* (New York, 2006)
Vargas, Claudia, *Antoni Gaudí: La arquitectura de la naturaleza* (Bogotá,
  2004)
Zerbst, Rainer, *Antoni Gaudí: A Life Devoted to Architecture,* trans. Doris
  Jones and Jeremy Gaines (London, 1985)

Articles

Bohigas, Oriol, 'Gaudí, entre Rusiñol y Dalí', *El País*, 8 January 2003

Burgen, Stephen, 'A Man on a Mission to Preserve Barcelona's Decorative Floor Tiles', *The Guardian*, 10 January 2022

Casanova, Rossend, 'Gaudí, puesto al día por Giralt-Miracle', *La Vanguardia*, 12 December 2012

Dalí, Salvador, 'De la beauté terrifiante et comestible de l'architecture Modern'style', *Minotaure*, 3–4 (December 1933), pp. 69–76

Fernández, Víctor, 'Ricardo Opisso, el hombre que lo sabía todo sobre Gaudí', *La Razón*, 6 January 2021

Giralt-Miracle, Daniel, Introduction to Joan Bergós, *Gaudí: L'home i l'obra* (Barcelona, 1999), pp. 9–10

Glancey, Jonathan, 'Gaudí's La Sagrada Família: Genius or Folly', BBC Culture, www.bbc.com, 21 October 2014

Graell, Vanessa, 'El modernismo surrealista de Jujol', *El Mundo*, 14 February 2014

Hornblower, Margot, 'My Client Isn't in Any Hurry', *Time*, 19 November 1990, pp. 64–5

Hughes, Robert, 'A Hulking, Delirious Beauty', *The Guardian*, 10 October 2007

Jacobs, Michael, 'Gaudí Mania', *Art Quarterly* (Summer 2002), pp. 48–53

Mackay, David, 'Searching for a New Language in the Past', in *Barcelona: Metròpolis mediterrània*, 58 (2002)

Moore, Rowan, 'Sagrada Família: Gaudí's Cathedral is Nearly Done, but Would He Have Liked It?' *The Observer*, 24 April 2011

Morgades, Lourdes, 'La Sagrada Família de la discordia', *El País*, 8 July 1990

Solà-Morales, Ignasi de, 'Modernista Architecture', in *Homage to Barcelona: The City and Its Art, 1888–1936*, ed. Marilyn McCully (London, 1986), pp. 115–31

Part Two: General Books with Content Relating to Gaudí

Boyd, Alastair, *The Essence of Catalonia* (London, 1988)

Burton, Richard, *Prague: A Cultural and Literary History* (Oxford, 2003)

Cirici, Alexandre, *Barcelona pam a pam* (Barcelona, 1971)

Dearden, James, *John Ruskin* (Kettering, n.d.)

Eaude, Michael, *Catalonia: A Cultural History* (Oxford, 2007)

—, *Sails and Winds* (Oxford, 2019)

Farràs, Andreu, *Els Güell* (Barcelona, 2016)

Fleming, John, et al., *The Penguin Dictionary of Architecture* (London, 1972)

Ford, Richard, *Handbook for Spain 1845* (Arundel, 1966), vol. II, pp. 689–769

Goytisolo, Juan, *Aproximaciones a Gaudí en Capadocia* (Madrid, 1990)

Hughes, Robert, *Barcelona* (London, 1992)

Jacobs, Michael, *Barcelona* (Blue Guide) (London, 1991)

Langdon-Davies, John, *Gatherings from Catalonia* (London, 1953)

Macaulay, Rose, *Fabled Shore* (London, 1949)

McCully, Marilyn, ed., *Homage to Barcelona: The City and Its Art, 1888–1936* (London, 1986)

Mackay, David, *Modern Architecture in Barcelona, 1854–1939* (Sheffield, 1985)

—, *A Life in Cities* (Edinburgh, 2009)

Martínez, Guillem, *Barcelona rebelde* (Barcelona, 2009)

Mendoza, Eduardo, and Cristina Mendoza, *Barcelona modernista* (Barcelona, 1989)

Morris, Jan, *Spain* (London, 2008)

Orwell, George, *Homage to Catalonia* (London, 1970)

Payne, John, *Catalonia: History and Culture* (Nottingham, 2004)

Pevsner, Nikolaus, *Pioneers of Modern Design* (London, 1970)

Terry, Arthur, *A Literary History of Spain: Catalan Literature* (London, 1972)

Tóibín, Colm, *Homage to Barcelona* (London, 1994)

Trenc Ballester, Eliseu, and Alan Yates, *Alexandre de Riquer* (Sheffield, 1988)

Novels

Serge, Victor, *Birth of Our Power* (London, 1977)

Wilson, Barbara, *Gaudí Afternoon* (London, 1991)

Films

Alaimo, John, dir., *Antonio Gaudí, una visión inacabada* (1974)

Antonioni, Michelangelo, dir., *The Passenger* (1975); with scenes in the Palau Güell and on the roof of the Casa Milà

Huerga, Manuel, dir., *Gaudí* (1989)

Seidelman, Susan, dir., *Gaudí Afternoon* (2001)

Teshigahara, Hiroshi, dir., *Antonio Gaudí* (1984)

Acknowledgements

More people than I can mention have contributed over the years to whatever understanding I may have of Catalonia and Gaudí. The following have assisted me, in several and varied ways, specifically with this book: Brian Anglo, Jordi Carruesco (Torre Bellesguard), Pilar Delgado (Casa Vicens), Carolina García Estévez (Serra Húnter Professor, Polytechnic University of Barcelona), Dámaso Martín Martín (photographer and expert in Barcelona's architecture), Antonio Oliva Sacristán (Casa Vicens) and Berta Pfaff (Torre Bellesguard).

Photo Acknowledgements

The author and publishers wish to express their thanks to the sources listed below for illustrative material and/or permission to reproduce it.

Marisa Asensio: pp. 8, 10 (with kind permission of the Catalana Occidente Insurance Company: www.bellesguardgaudi.com), 22, 40, 47, 62, 64, 66, 73, 74, 76, 100, 101, 111, 112, 114, 115, 119 (with kind permission of the Catalana Occidente Insurance Company: www.bellesguard.com), 121, 123, 124 top and bottom, 125, 129, 132, 133, 137, 138, 140, 142, 145 (with kind permission of the Fundació Catalunya La Pedrera), 146 (with kind permission of the Fundació Catalunya La Pedrera), 160, 172, 174, 176, 177; courtesy Museu Salvador Vilaseca, Reus: p. 28 (photo Pau Audouard & Company, Barcelona); Sebastian Ballard: p. 12; Josep Brangulí (*Gaseta de les Arts*, 1 July, 1926): p. 106; Feliu Elias (Apa): p. 157; Dámaso Martín: pp. 24, 52, 87, 90; Courtesy of the Fundació Enric Miralles: p. 170; Quelus (courtesy of Gijs van Hensbergen): p. 165; Wikimedia Commons: pp. 14 (Jordi Gili/CC BY-SA 4.0/converted to b&w), 50 (Public Domain), 69 (Triplecaña/CC BY-SA 4.0/converted to b&w), 102 (Pau Audouard Deglaire/Public Domain), 154 (Public Domain), 156 (Josep Brangulí/Public Domain).